Paths
The fight for honour.

Lee Mayo

as told to Simon Morrell

Copyright © 2022 Lee Mayo

All rights reserved.

ISBN:
9798367591170

DEDICATION

I knew on some level I needed to change my life around but none of us can do that on our own and so Paths is for the following people who helped steer my ship back to shore.
Charlotte, Hannah, Crystal, Max, Bella and of course my nephew Rhys Masterson.

Lee Mayo

SIMON MORRELL

Simon is the award-winning author of the true stories 'From Bullied to Black Belt' and the sequel 'An Everyday Warrior'.

His feature film script "Being Bullied" is currently under development as a British film.

He has also penned another four books and currently runs The Storytellers, from which he writes and publishers books for people with tales to tell, but they aren't sure how to go about it.

If you have a story you would like him to consider then go to www.simonmorrell.com and make contact from there.

"I'll bring the whiskey, you tell me your story."

Simon Morrell.

Paths

A true story as told by Lee Mayo to Simon Morrell.

Certain names and events have been changed to protect innocent people and, in some cases, for illustration purposes.

Today's Mental Health Issues.

As it stands today, one in six people will suffer from mental health problems and that is just in the United Kingdom. In 2019, again in the U.K. 5,691 took their own lives after suffering similar problems.

With the best will in the world the experts, professionals and NHS are failing people.

Whilst the powers that be eat in fancy establishments and doctors dole out humbug pills, people are dying. People are taking their own lives.

We need better from those who are supposed to provide it. We deserve better. Joe deserved better.

What you are about to read is a true story of a man's fight for his friend.

*Source ons.gov.uk. National statistics.

Prologue

I try not to let the holidaymakers distract me, but it is hard, for my God do they make a racket. Not even on the plane yet and the kids are screaming for ice cream, mums for a brandy to calm pre-flight nerves and the dads? Well, the dads just want a cold pint, a well-deserved one after a year of toil in the workplace.

A cold pint though is the furthest thing on my mind. I'm in good shape, I know it. Months of training and years of fighting make it that way. I also know I must be because the guy waiting for me at the end of my, soon-to-board flight, well he may have a drink with me after our business, but not before and certainly not during.

I'm distracted by the intercom calling my ride out.

Heathrow to Bangkok is eleven hours and thirty minutes if you are counting, and I will be, every second of the way. Mind tricks can do that to you, one minute the time flies (no pun intended readers), and the next thing it is like watching paint dry.

I take my seat, the window one this time and I'm aware that the guy occupying the seat next to me isn't whom I want him to be. It isn't who it should be at all.

However, I politely nod to my fellow passengers, all scrummaging to be first off, the plane, first in the bar, and first in the pool. Lucky bastards. Lucky because their time in Thailand will be much easier than mine.

Mine will be a painful one, both painful physically and mentally.

Painfully because the guy I am going to meet will attempt to remove my limbs, all eight of them in the Thai Boxing ring. Mentally because, well just because that's what these things are. These journeys into the arena are always mentally so very tough, tough enough to break most men.

It hasn't broken me though. Over the years it's come close. This world I chose, the world I found myself in had almost been too much for me but break me it did not.

I watch as the rain bounced off the tarmac and although aware of the background noise, the excited families and the loudspeakers instructing us to put our seatbelts on I find myself lost in thought a little.

Why was I doing this, what was the point? The answer to both these questions makes me emotionally because the answer is obvious. It is Joe, the guy who should be in the seat next to me. It is Joe I'm doing this for because Joe isn't here to do it for himself.

Joe isn't here because Joe took his own life and that makes me angry, it makes me sad, it makes me determined. I'm bringing the title back home for Joe, that you can take to the bank.

One other question though, one that is on repeat all the time.

How did I get to this point, what drew me all the way here?

And now I'm about to share the answer with you, an answer that is obvious all along.

Chapter One

Kids can be cruel, it's not a nasty thing it is just what they do, but that doesn't mean it doesn't hurt.

The clothes I wear are made with loving hands, the hands of my Nan but these lot don't care.

"Wurzel," they yell. "Hey Wurzel Gummidge! Your jumper has more holes than the crazy golf on the prom." They are of course comparing me to the television scarecrow and why not? My clothes are of a similar fashion and sometimes I feel like I wouldn't be at home in a field somewhere, scaring the crap out of the little buggers.

As the rest of the gang join in the laughter, my ears burn with shame but I'm damned if I'll let them see and so I shrug it off. I try to ignore it because all I can see is my Nan knitting away whilst my mum is somewhere else uninterested, not willing to chip in herself. I won't see it yet, not for many years, but when I do her culpable behavior as a negligent mum will hurt. It will hurt but it will benefit me as I vow to never be *that parent* to my own children.

The rags, the poverty, and the lifestyle (ha, if you can call it that), would drive me in other ways later in life. The adversity would provide fuel, inspiration, drive, and a backbone to do better.

I would find much success in worlds I was happy to thrive in and in worlds, well worlds that maybe I shouldn't have chosen to enter anyway but as they say, "he without sin cast the first stone."

Before all this though, I would have to endure. Oh yes, I would have to endure, and I saw things a kid shouldn't see.

I would have to endure the walk of shame to school in the poor man's clothes, only to make the return walk home to a house full of vicious skinheads, with heads in the glue pot only taking a break from the aroma of solvents to partake in the smoking of drugs.

My sister Angela reluctantly hosts the parties as she shares my harsh lifestyle and I come to realise, maybe this is her way of coping with how we live. Maybe the party life and the people who fill our house are her escapism, this, her days at senior school and of course, her beloved moped.

Angela will prove to be a good sister though, looking out for me as a young'un.

Even though we had different dads, we shared the same surname, that of her father and this was a source of resentment for me. I was named after a man I wasn't even related to and so when the time came, I changed my back to the surname of my mum as I felt more connected to them, my u John in particular.

Still, though she looked after me even she bore the brunt of my wild side.

One afternoon whilst she was elsewhere, I decided to take her moped for a spin, prizing open the box that housed the clocks so I could hotwire the engine.

Kickstarting the thing, I took to riding the streets like Phil Daniels from Quadrophenia. Only I wasn't. The only thing that came rushing to my face was the tarmac as I lost control and smashed into the pavement, bashing up the bodywork and mudguard.

As I pushed it home, I prayed the bollocking she would give me would be quick and painless if not thoroughly deserved.

My worries were for nothing as poor Angela blamed herself. She herself had suffered the same fate as me the night before, crashing in the pitch dark.

It was that darkness that saved me as she thought she had caused the damage but didn't see it in the night sky. Still, that is what sisters are for isn't it?

Mopeds aside, the parties and the company though became the norm in our house as our dear mum not only turned a blind eye to it all but treated it as the status quo. It was no wonder I was heading down the path of criminality, self-destruction, and a life on the dark side, accompanied by darker people than myself.

I craved a father figure, a dad like all the other kids in school had but he was as likely to turn up as a new pair of shoes, decent pants, and a shirt that fitter, but that was okay. For now, I didn't know him and apparently, he sure as hell didn't want to know me. How wrong I was, but I found out too late.

I met him later in life, now a dad myself and he was not the dad my mum had poisoned me to.

The biggest tragedy was that just as I was getting to know him, just as I became aware of what a great man he was, he passed away from a disease and it was heart-breaking.

But from his death I took one great thing; for all the bad-mouthing my mum had done, for all the slagging, ripping and betraying him as some sort of monster, my dad passed without once scurrying her name. Never did I hear him say a bad word about her and trust me, it would have been justified.

Instead, just as I was getting to know him, he was gone, but long before that, the man who took his place was a man with his own troubles, my Uncle John.

Drugs can take down any man, don't be fooled otherwise. The only true escape from their clutches is to not start using at all, but don't we wish we were all so clever? So no, don't be pulled into the grip of them, especially the hard stuff. Avoid it like the plague but sadly my surrogate dad couldn't do that.

He became hooked on heroin, using which then led to dealing. That in turn led to a hefty fucking spell inside, a guest of her majesty, but the pleasure he took from drugs eventually turned out to be none.

On the face of it, he was living the high life and the benefits that go with being a big player in the drug dealing world.

When I was just eight years old, I was aware the police were after him and he was now very well known to them, so much so that in their infinite wisdom, they saw fit to send him a Christmas card which read "See you next year." That little gem backfired as Uncle John produced it in a subsequent court case, clearly proving that although he was dealing, this was a definite example of police harassment.

Still, even at a such young age, I lived the high life

with my uncle, being ferried around in flash 'muscle' cars such as Audis and Jags, all top of the range and all impressive to a kid like me.

He would also turn up with high-end, expensive gifts that more than made up for the poverty I found myself living in. Televisions, Walkmans, keyboards and video players, stuff that cost more than we would see in a year and definitely out of our household's budget.

Uncle John became the best thing in my life, the man who taught me to ride a bike, the man who talked to me on a level that made me feel worth something and certainly the man who had my best interests at heart.

Despite his attention and his love, I was still bought up like some sort of vermin, something on the soles of someone's shoes like it was something they had stood in.

I would think nothing of hurling objects at neighbours who dared to tell me off for my behaviour. One, in particular, bore the brunt of a four-by-two piece of timber, launched at his head from a five-foot drop. How the hell was I to know this was wrong? Up to this point, my entertainment was a trip to the shops with a handwritten note, my mum's as she begged the shopkeeper to give me alcohol to take home. This was the era of 'turning a blind eye and I would inevitably trudge back up the road with a bottle of something for mum, and the sweets I stole for myself as when the shopkeeper turned his back to fetch the booze.

Living this kind of life, this kind of poverty and hardship can make you do things so out of character for a young boy. Looking back now as I bring up my own children the right way, I see that my behaviour wasn't right, but whom did I have to tell me I was going wayward?

I would think nothing of smashing up six-foot fences, running through to see if I could make it to the other side. Caring not a jot for my sister's well-being and so digging massive holes in the garden, covering these holes with long grass and laughing like a hyena when she chased me and ended up falling into the pit I had created.

To make matters worse, this resulted in my first police caution as I knew I had to hide the proceeds of that debris from that hole from my sister so she wouldn't cotton on as to my escapade, and so threw the lot over the fence. Little did I know at the time that over the other side of that fence lay the local police station. They were not a happy bunch to see bricks and rubble bring down a seven-foot tree and so it wasn't long before I first heard the knock on the door. Even at this very young age, I could tell this wouldn't be my first brush with the law. It was what it was.

As for my education, well this was well and truly the days of 'old school' and it was nothing for the headmaster to chase us in his car as we ducked and dived through alleyways, over fences and making it back to my friend's empty house for an afternoon of peace and quiet.

Our reward for this endeavour was a simple solution; a slap around the face from the said headmaster that would, these days produce a protest, mini-riot, and full police enquiry, but that was just how things were done back then.

Dealing with bullies, as far as I was concerned was done differently. I remember at some point, despite now being involved in, and getting good at Karate, getting 'bested' by a bully.

My solution to this, because I was damned if I was going to let the guy get the better of me, was to head for home a shift through my impressive collection of knives (thirty of them), an old-style policeman's truncheon and a set of nunchakus, and go back to the bully to take my vengeance.

This craziness was only highlighted by the fact my mum found my small arms cache when she moved the furniture and came across them hidden under the television. Instead of giving me a well-deserved, well-anticipated bollocking, she turned to my Uncle Phil and asked him to 'choose his weapon.'

He was involved in the skinhead's crack den and obviously needed a piece for protection. Who would have thought he would get it from my mum via her own son's box of tricks?

The madness would continue as I was so pissed off after an argument with my sister that I aimed a well-placed dart through the hole in her bedroom door (don't ask, some misdemeanour or other) and narrowly avoided blinding her in one eye.

This though, the incident with the dart? It was nothing compared to literally stabbing her in the back after a sibling's squabble. Thank God the blade was flimsy and didn't damage her in any way because it is a distinct possibility, I could have been looking at more than a police caution this time.

Looking back, it was no wonder I behaved this way.

Where were my parental guidance, my discipline, and the person to show me right from wrong? It certainly wasn't the guy barely knew, another one of my mum's fellas who dragged me from house to house, probably to give my mum some peace, but his chosen houses being drug dens or a room full of pissheads. Eight years old and living this kind of life. Imagine. It is best you don't. Just be grateful you are reading it from behind the safety of the pages in this book and not being on the front line of a life of madness.

Chapter Two

Through all that very madness of my childhood, certainly the very early years it seemed like my Uncle John was always on the peripheral, always trying on some level to look after me, but he had his own failings, and these were reinforced to me later in life when I visited him in prison.

He wasn't a tough guy, and it was through the grapevine that I heard he was being forced to smuggle drugs into prison. The black eye he sported on one visit would indicate he had, at some point, refused to do so but all that can change at the hands of another man's fist.

His reward for his antics, the antics he eventually had to agree to do (smuggle the drugs) was to be put in the most serious part of any jail, the Cat A section.

It was in one of these accommodations, Wayland prison in Norwich that he pointed out to me one of Britain's most notorious villains, Ronnie Biggs, the great train robber.

So, whilst other kids were getting their treats by trips to Disney World, or camping in France with their parents, I was being shunted from one jail to the next, visiting one rogue or another and gradually forming the belief that this was what life had in store for me, this was my future. A life like Uncle John.

I always wondered why my mum let someone who was clearly an addict to take care of me but that didn't stop me from loving him and my weekend spent at his home.

An absent dad leaves a massive hole to fill and Uncle John filled it the best he could with love, kindness and attention. He also did something that was to change my life forever: introduced me to Bruce Lee.

Karate and Martial Arts here I came. It was a path that led me to glory and yet further down the road was my key into the dark world.

Sundays for me growing up in Southend on Sea were not about trips to the seaside. There was no money for the arcades, no time for sandcastles and certainly, we couldn't afford the dosh to visit Peter Pan's Playground, a theme park that sat at the north end of the town's pier, but what we could do was what most kids in this era spent their time and money doing. scanning the movies at the local video store.

Before re-inventing itself later on in time, with all

sorts of fancy sound equipment and brilliant visual displays, cinemas would take a back seat at this time as we bought Hollywood into our very own front rooms. So, when I say Uncle John introduced me to Bruce, I'm not saying we shook hands amongst the fisherman's huts and the world's largest pier, but he did pop into my front room occasionally.

His Enter the Dragon had me spellbound, Game of Death had me thinking I wanted to be like Bruce and Fists of Fury only reinforced that belief.

Other films would be our entertainment as Uncle John and I continued to bond but it was the flying kicks, badly dubbed sound and crunching of bones that held me captive.

But before I would enter a dojo for the first time, a wide-eyed six-year-old who had never felt accomplishment, before that happened, I would dread the end of those lovely weekends and my return home to my house of thorns.

Returning to my neglectful mother, allowing my childhood to slip into a life of bunking off school and the inevitable decline into sniffing glue, just like I saw the skinheads do at the parties my mother allowed at the family home.

I'm not sure I felt shame just yet, but I knew there

was certainly something not right about this boy's life.

Karate was the change that, like Karate had changed the lives of so many before me and the hordes of people that followed me into it.

At six years old a kid should have some idea of basic discipline, a way of behaving and respecting others. I don't think I had that, I was still vandalising, still sniffing from the left-over glue bags and yes, the fights at school were all part and parcel of this undisciplined kid's life. All that was about to change.

If you have ever walked into a dojo, you will know straight away the feelings I had, the very ones I am going to describe.

This six-year-old, this young Lee Mayo, known as coming from the house of mayhem, walked into the dojo and I didn't know if I was joining a religious cult or there to learn how to fight, and by that, I mean fight the correct way.

The instructor took me under his wing straight away. I have no idea of his background. Was his dad absent? Did his mum encourage the local young warriors to party their life away in his front room?

How about this? Had he ever taken substances even

if just to get away from it all? I don't know and at my young age, it didn't matter.

What mattered was he gave me respect, he gave me focus, and he gave me a healthy way to 'escape'. And yes, he gave me press-ups. Lots of them.

There is purpose in a dojo if you are willing to accept it, no matter how young or old you are.

This man was showing me a way forward, a way to behave and I was to take to it, but not just yet.

The physical skills, the kicks, punches, blocks and sparring were the easy part. It was the boundaries that go with it I couldn't understand.

Karate was, is a *way*. It is a way to be better, a way to live, a way to gain and to get respect but that wasn't going to happen for me if I couldn't lose this bitter skin I had chosen to wear.

School life took a new meaning for me.

"You don't like the clothes I wear? No problem, take this roundhouse kick to your head and wipe that fucking smirk off your face." Bang, the kid goes down. Easy.

"What were you saying about the holes in my shoes? Here, take a closer look and join your buddy on the floor," and my foot makes contact yet again, this one is easier than the first. It's easier because I am starting to enjoy myself.

"Next!" I almost declare until I am fighting on a daily basis, drawing attention to myself except I come to realise it isn't the type of attention I crave. It is however the type of attention cruel schoolteachers like to dish out.

With the damage done and kids battered the powers that be in the school contacted the powers that be in the Karate dojo and I was bought before the instructor. He was a scary guy, heaped in traditional values and let me know in no uncertain terms that my behaviour was unacceptable.

I wasn't used to this sort of discipline, I had free reign over my world and could do what I wanted, come and go as I pleased, but this rude awakening was probably needed.

However, he then went off the record and gave me another piece of advice, and this too was welcomed because I had never experienced any praise. He congratulated me for defending myself having been the brunt of such bullying and ridicule because of our poverty. He was pleased that I had applied in real life what he had taught me on the wooden floors of his dojo, so the praise I received was most welcome, but there was another dark cloud on the horizon; I had developed a taste for violence and there was a group of people on hand to take me on board, make me one of their own and expose me to the real stuff, real street fighting, not playground tussles.

The skinheads that had inhabited my mum's house, those bald fighters with a diet of glue, drugs and violence had come to see me as a mascot, but not the type to sit pitch side and cheer the main players on.

No, they wanted their young 'un right in the thick of it and so that is where I went. I was out to impress my new tribe, my extended family.

My mum had taken to piecing everybody in our street. Now think about health and safety in the modern-day world and then see my mum as something completely opposite.

Burning her needle on the old stove was enough to satisfy her that it was safe, and off she went poking holes here, there, and everywhere. Five of them into her own seven-year-old son's ear.

Should she have pieced my ears at such a young age and in such a dangerous way? Probably not, but then she probably shouldn't have sent that same seven-year-old off to war, a Bank Holiday Southend war with his tribe doing battle with Mods, Punks and any fucker that looked different to us.

There would be other gang fights in my life, but nothing fills the pants with buckets of shit like your first one, certainly not at such a young age.

Sixteen- to twenty-year-olds 'legging' us armed with bricks from skips, pieces of wood equipped full of nails, anything they could use to damage us and fuck it if you were just a kid.

You chose, at such a wise and wonderful age to 'get involved' and now you were, so 'run young boy, run.'

It was an introduction to real violence that would ironically serve me well later on in life.

It was now obvious my mum was a control freak and, in an effort, to escape her clutches, if just for a few short hours, I planned a trip out in my Datsun Sunny, ironically the car she bought me for passing my test. However, in her ever-present controlling manner she confiscated the keys so I couldn't get out and about.

I wouldn't be thwarted and went under the dash and wired the car to make my escape, but even this strike out for independence hit a brick wall.

I stopped for petrol and without thinking turned the car off. Of course, as soon as I had filled up and needed to head off again, I realised I didn't have any keys and so, like a 1970's American cop show got back under the dash for the hot wire trick again. Only this time I was caught.

Fortune favours the brave and, in this case, my act of bravery in escaping mum's clutches via a car thief's trick turned out to be getting caught by a guy who would become a massive influence in my life. Enter Mr Dave Burnett, a mechanic of the old school who really knew his stuff. I was introduced to Dave the week before by my cousin as we were out and about.

Now, remember Dave had only met me once in a pub when we just said hello to one another and the next time he sees me I'm on a forecourt hot wiring a car. Not a good look at all and one Dave picked up on.

"What the bloody hell are you doing?" he growled at me. "Are you stealing this?"

I think I must have stuttered and stammered, maybe even redden at the situation.

"No, no nothing like that. I just can't get my car started," I offered in response.

I went on to explain how mum had bought me the car for passing my test but now hid my keys as she didn't want me going out.

I think Dave rolled his eyes in what looked like a mad excuse but eventually believed me and went on to become a big part of my life, all through the fate of a controlling mother.

However, Dave 'the mission man' was never one for conformity and in true fashion, later on in life when we had become friends, he called me an early afternoon to enquire about my plans for that evening.

Now sometimes I'll have a quick pint after work, but Dave had other ideas.

"Pack your bags," he told me, "I've got you a ticket to Tenerife. We leave later today." And so began the Tenerife adventures I talk about later on in this book.

However, the biggest and most beautiful lesson I learnt from my mum was that my own kids, my own beautiful children would never live this life. Not whilst I still had breath in me.

Chapter Three

There are two types of fighting, so some people will say. There is the hooliganism of the football terraces (though even these guys leave out 'civilians), the savagery of a tear-up on a Bank Holiday Monday and these are all related to the brawls after closing time, the smashed windows, screaming girls and blood on the pavement.

Then there is what can be known as 'honest fighting.' A straightener between two sworn enemies, who believe it all not, after the swinging punches and brutal headbutts stop, become the best of buddies. It's more common than you think.

This is an arranged match, a mutual understanding that this fight matters, it has a history, a background and therefore some justification.

And sitting on the branches of the same family tree, there is the sport fighting. Muay Thai, Karate, Boxing, Wrestling, men with honour, men who show respect.

And this was my first 'respectful fight.'

My Uncle John really stepped up for me at this point. I was now living with him at the weekends as my mum had other things on, probably things I shouldn't have been a part of. The house was now a party house, not the ideal environment for a young boy, certainly not as I was developing a taste for fighting and the rewards that could easily sway me one way or another.

I was now hanging about with the skinheads, my sister and her friends, all considerably older than me and so Uncle john took me in at the weekend and then surprised me with my first-ever holiday, a trip to Holland.

Unfortunately, the date clashed with my first formal fight, a Karate tournament and I was desperate to compete in it. Telling my mum was always going to be a difficult thing to do and her reaction was one of anger.

Grabbing me by the collar, she marched me up to the top of our road, pushing me into the old red phone box and insisted it was me who told Uncle John I didn't want to go with him, all whilst telling me how ungrateful I was. I didn't need telling, even at that early age I know what I was, but nothing was going to stop me from fighting.

My heart started pounding as I dreaded the call that would follow and sure enough, after a few seconds I heard Uncle John's voice greet me.

"Hello Lee, my son. Are you looking forward to Holland? We will have a great time."

I remember feeling both sick and defiant, Holland could wait. Seconds passed before I could find the right words.

"Uncle John, I don't want to go with you. I've got a chance to enter a tournament and I want to fight."

I think I heard a resigned sigh from him as he took this in. Of course, his first reaction was the try and change my mind.

"Lee pal, you have never had a holiday. Look the break will be good for you, we will have a great time just the two of us."

Even though he couldn't see me, I was shaking my head furiously as my mum watched on, both angry and I guess sad for Uncle John.

"No Uncle John. I don't want to go, I want to fight," I repeated. "I don't mean to sound ungrateful, but I just don't want to go with you this time."

My best Uncle John showed his colours.

"Lee, if that is what you want to do, then do it. Who am I to stop you? There will be other times, but if you are going to fight, you do your best to win. Do you hear me son?"

This time my head shaking turned to nods, even though I could still feel disappointment radiating from my mum.

"I will Uncle John. I'm sorry," I muttered.

"I wish I could be there for you Lee, but I can't cancel my holiday now."
I understood and knew it would be unfair of him to do so.

As we walked back down the road, back to our home, the frosty silence was broken by my mum uttering her own words.

"You better fucking win something after wasting your uncle's money. You are turning into a fucking horrible kid. This had better be worth it or...", she didn't finish her sentence, but I knew what she meant.

I didn't disappoint. Coming second in Kata (pre-arranged moves) was a great feeling, but it didn't compare to coming first in Kumite (fighting) and it would be the first Gold I ever won. It wouldn't be the last.

Chapter Four

If suffering at home, if the one thing made all the poverty worthwhile it was Karate. Here I was, this rag-tag kid from a house that seemed to bring me nothing but misery (and lots of holes in my ears) and suddenly I have found a way, I have found my way.

I was getting good at dishing out the hidings to the cheeky little fuckers at school, but where was the benefit in that? All that did was bring more grief, and I was carrying enough of that.

A mum who referred to me as a 'fucking horrible kid,' a dad nowhere to be seen and a home full of skinheads keen to both look after me and exploit me. Sure, I had a great man in my uncle and my sister was always there for me, but the rest of the stuff was bringing me down.

You don't realise it at the time, but it does. Even if somewhere in the back of your mind you think "this is no way for a boy to live," you don't come out and admit it, even to yourself and so you plod on until you find something that is yours and so here I was.

"Lee Mayo!" I heard the shout and looked up to see my Karate Instructor approach.

"Yes Sensei?" I responded with all the respect I

could muster.

"Lee, you are ready for your next grading. It will take place in two weeks so you will have to put in extra hours and sharpen yourself up a bit but you are ready. You are flying son."

He patted my shoulders and walked away, leaving me ten feet tall.

Of course, I would put the required time in. What else was I going to do? Spend the hours sniffing glue or watching others get high from whatever they were taking?

Suddenly the ten press-ups I can manage aren't enough and I rocking out twenty.

You can't keep up with my sit-ups because this boy now has the bug.

This 'Karate lark' as some people called it, was my way out. Even at this young age I was getting respect, being recognised, and being part of a team, not hell-bent on destruction or violence.

In true 'young Lee' fashion, it wouldn't last. I mean why would it?

Other than Uncle John, the only man I had truly looked up to was my Instructor and I turned up for training one day to find him gone. No reasons why, no goodbye, no explanation other than "politics Lee, you are too young to understand."

And they were right. I didn't understand and truth be told I didn't want to understand. Why would I? I was just a kid whose role model and simply gone, and seemingly with him any dreams of a Karate life.

Two other people turned up to take his place, a guy and a girl God love them, and they would try but that feeling a fighter gets when he is 'home' had disappeared.

If the home had gone from here then I needed to man up and find a new one. After all, don't we all move houses in our lives?

Despite the rumours telling me it was a tough club, I made the move up the road to train under Head Coach Steve Quinn and England Karate International Steve Scarrott. This was a place where it was alleged nobody would go because you would "get bashed up," but I loved it.

The two coaches were well known in Essex as being tough guys and stood on the doors of the area's clubs, forging and enforcing that reputation. They were serious men and not to be messed with but where I was concerned, they took me under their wing, taking me along to summer camps and tournaments.

I loved it, it was like having a new family. A healthy influence that was driving me toward, and then through my teenage years.

My earlier glue sniffing days were replaced with tough training sessions, which in turn were rewarded with a success a Southend kid like me never even dreamed of. Donning the white suits of Karate (gi) gave me purpose, but it also gave me success.

Along the way I had to take a punch to give two, endure a kick to the stomach to land my own to my opponent's head, always searching for the Holy Grail of the 'Ippon", the highest single point you can score in Karate and untimely called 'the Killing Blow!"

These Ippons soon added up and it seemed like people were pointing at me and commenting "that's Lee Mayo, English and British Karate Champion."

Pats on the back were followed with the question, "Are you really on the English Ishin-Ryu Karate team?"

My answer was "yes," and it was all done under Karate legend Sensei Ticky Donovan O.B.E. and 10th Dan Black Belt.

Sensei Donovan had done the lot. British Champion

in'73, '74 and again in 1974, he added to his glory years by being part of the World Champions team also in 1975.

He would go on to become the British team coach with consecutive World Championship titles in '82, '84, '86, '88 and Mexico in 1990.

You have to understand that these titles were all the more respected when you realise they were all won 'away from home'. That is on foreign soil. It is hard enough fighting at your local sports center on a Sunday afternoon, but to travel across the world to fight in an unknown place against an unknown opponent (s). Well that is a massive task and one I would find out just how hard to do many years later when I board that plane to Thailand.

For now, it was enough to know that having just graded under Sensei Donovan to 2nd Dan Black Belt, I was in the company of true warriors.

Chapter Five

Holding a Black Belt (a good one anyway) gives you respect and there are two types of this. Self-respect and the respect of others. The respect of others I enjoyed but the first kind, self-respect? Well, now that beauty was growing into a beast, starting to get out of control and turning into arrogance. In short, I was getting too confident, and any 'real fighter' can tell you, that's almost as bad, as damaging as having no or little confidence at all.

It switches us off, we are oblivious to the threats our opponent poses. We know lots, they know little. This semi-arrogance usually rewards us and not all rewards are shiny and good.

My friend was training in Kickboxing and was pestering me to go along.

"You will fit right in Lee, you're a Black Belt so what have you got to be frightened of?" Famous last words, almost.

So away I went, off and up another path ad found myself in a club that was largely beginners. My previous experiences gave me an age over the newcomers, even though they were training to fight full-contact in the ring.

As I trained alongside them the coach asked me if I

wanted to fight in the forthcoming Kickboxing show and of course, I said yes. I'd take my Black Belt skills into the ring, and it should be a comfortable night out.

"Oh Lee," I now say to myself, shaking my head and with a wry grin on my face. "What were you thinking?"

It became clear early on in the fight that my point-scoring skills were not welcome here, would not do me any good inside these damn ropes, and that my Black Belt had been left outside the ring.

Three rounds can feel like thirty when you are getting the crap kicked out of you.

"What is this Wizardry this boy is throwing? Where are the straight 'pulled' punches to my body? Why isn't the ref stopping to award points every time I throw my own shots and just what the hell are these weird circular punches that keep removing me from my senses? Oh, uppercuts and hooks? Right, not seen these before."

To compound my misery, I learnt after the fight that my victor had only been training for six months, a baby compared with the years and shifts I had put in.

So, in my sorry state, I conceded that Karate didn't

work (sacrilege, under the right circumstances it does indeed work), and as I licked my wounds, I considered my future.

I had just been 'bested' by a Kickboxer, so what do from here?

Why become one myself, that's what do! And so that is what I did!

My teenage years were moving fast and I was turning into a young man. As the years passed, I found more and more that I was in the Kickboxing ring rather than places full of wrong 'uns taking the bad stuff. Days of letting my mum poke holes in my ears were a thing of the past and I had learned to transfer my Karate skills into full contact bouts, round after round, fight after fight and what is more important in my eyes, winning those fights. Life was good, life was fighting fit.

There I saw another step up, or certainly I different approach.

I was watching a bout and witnessed some buggers elbow and knee each other as well as dishing punishment via the usual fists and feet.

"Well Lee," I said to myself (again). "Looks like you have to change tactics and make another switch."

And so, a Thai Boxer did I become. It was life-changing, as so many of my Martial Art years had been. It was also going to change the company I kept although I didn't see that coming at the time. No, those adventures would be for later.

I was starting to look after myself and the fitter and physically stronger I became, the mentally better I was.

I felt as though something was missing, a piece of the jigsaw that didn't quite fit. I soon realised what it was; I was too skinny. It was time to 'beef up.'

There were lots of places in Southend to take to lifting weights, but my choice of poison was 'Smarts', a great local place run by a top bloke. Mike Williams was a professional bodybuilder and so good at it that they named a show after him, the 'Mike Williams Classic.' In the world of bodybuilding, to have a show named after you is an honour.

I would train at the gym and at the same time watch in awe as these guys piled on the plates and developed bodies to be proud of. My Martial Arts, and in a particular my Thai Kickboxing world was still my number one priority but bodybuilding was a way of building the armour, putting muscle on to protect the fighting skills I was honing.

It was another piece of good fortune for me that Mike found out I was a fighter and took me under his wing. By now my lack of a father so far in life had been made up for with the likes of the two Steves and now Mike being my mentors, and then my pals.

Mike was the head doorman at some big London clubs such as the Milk Bar which stood on the corner of Charing Cross Road. It kept good company being directly opposite the famous Astoria club and the Velvet Underground.

It was sad to see the Astoria demolished in 2009 as it was the place that launched many great British bands and hosted plenty of international stars including the Beach Boys, U2 and Prince to name a few, but progress is progress and today it is no longer, instead the site is part of the Crossrail development.

The Milk Bar was owned by the famous d.j. Nicky Holloway but the doors were run by Tony Tucker, who was well known for being in the Essex Boys Gang and would go on to be brutally murdered in what became known as the Range Rover Murders, making national and international news years later.

For now, though it was his club which would give you some indication of how respected, and maybe feared Mike was to head his door.

So, when Mike offered me a job on the door I was absolutely buzzing. Not only was the extra money welcome but it opened a whole new world to me. I would say opened lots of new doors but that would be a pun too far.

I was just twenty years of age when I donned the black and whites and snazzy bow tie but boy was I ready for it.

I had bulked up by now, but next to these guys I saw myself as 'small.' These fuckers were giants. Don't let anybody tell you 'size is an accident at birth.' This was no accident, these guys worked and worked hard for their status and now I was with them, I was 'in.'

However, being with them also exposed me to really hard-core people and their stories and persona make great 'after-hours, drinking with your buddies' tales.

One that sticks to mind is when Dave Courtney, a real London character and alleged gangster provided dancers to West Ham Football Club for their Christmas party. The club had hired the Milk Bar, the whole venue and the night was in full swing. If you have ever seen a footballers' party, well then you will know exactly what the scene would look like.

Fancy suits and watches, beautiful women and enough drink flowing to sink a ship.

Talking of fancy suits Dave was dressed in a flash one of his own and so one of the players, England International and future Manchester United player Rio Ferdinand decided to take liberties, really against a man he should have known better than to do that to. Rio approached Dave, and with a growing audience to match his ego sarcastically asked "Who are you? The fucking ice cream man?"

Dave kept his cool and simply replied, "How are you going to play in tomorrow's match son with a fucking big hole in your kneecap?"

Rio got the message and backed off, leaving Dave to his night as he looked to enjoy his own.

The short and few, but very carefully chosen words Dave used were enough to persuade our superstar to find someone else to harass and whilst he did play in the next game, I think maybe his mind wasn't on it and the man of the match award went to someone else. Dave could have that effect on people with his massive personality.

Fear can play a massive part in your life on the door, but only if you let it. Nowadays, with the creation of the S.I.A. and the door badges sometimes funded by the job centre, we see a different breed of a door supervisor. Even the title is different as some see the term 'bouncer' as an offensive one, but effectively that is what we were. If you misbehaved in our club (or any club for that matter) you were 'bounced' (out of the door.)

Nobody wants to see violence, and nobody wants to be part of it, but with a society and nightclub scene that invariably attracts a certain clientele then the door team needs to be capable of dealing with threats, threats that are more often than not carried out (or attempted to be carried out). These can include knives, firearms, and all sorts of weapons.

Sadly with people being forced onto the S.I.A. training programs to get them licensed and into work, sometimes these people might be best placed elsewhere. They are simply not built for the shit that can be thrown at them and their fear can cause all sorts of problems for them.

Luckily for me, I never had that issue on the door. I certainly felt it in the early Karate days. I'm just sixteen years old and facing battles with grown men who don't ask or give any quarter. No matter what your age, if you were game enough to step into the fight arena, then you had to be game enough to take your lumps. Simple as that. And so, my exposure to fear came as an adolescent, having already seen violence at a very early age with the skins on

Southend prom, this was just an extension of what I knew The fight arena very quickly became my church, the blood slit my prayers.

It would serve me well when the doors came along because I had grown so used to feeling my fear and then controlling that fear to go on and win big on the Karate stage, that 'real fighting' was just another step on my path.

This was despite dealing with football hooligans, heavy in numbers and high on substances or individuals equipped with and prepared to use the aforementioned weapons.

Fighting men in Karate suits on a Sunday afternoon at some national sports centre or men in bomber jackets on a Saturday night in a dangerous city centre just went hand in hand.

The stare out.

Kicking to victory.

Practice makes…

The winner…

Young Skins

And a strong door team

On the doors again.

My good friend Nipper.

Dave C and friends.

With Dave Lea

Chapter Six

Looking back now, older and wiser I realised I had some lucky escapes, but once the adrenalin kicks in, survival is everything. Things that now seem horrendous incidents were all just in a night's work.

The guy approaching the door wielding a machete? Well of course he is, why wouldn't he do that, so it is just the norm to jump on him, pin him to the floor and try and disarm him?

The trouble is the big bastard has it in the hand I am not pinning and is keeping it out of my reach behind his back.

My mate Steve, Ferguson fellow doorman and backup for the night watches on as I look like I am auditioning for Wrestle-mania, but it is far from a television show.

"Steve! The knife Steve!" I shout at my buddy. "Get the knife!"

Now tonight is the night Steve is oblivious.

"What?" he asks.

"Jesus! The knife Steve! Take the knife off him!" All this is said whilst I am still grappling for a submission, but this fucker is far from taping out.

Steve cottons on thank God.

"Bloody hell!" he shouts before grabbing the knife from my new dancing partner. Wrestle mania or Dancing on Ice, you decide.

Consequence. Consequence is a big word and an even bigger thing to deal with. Sometimes the consequences of our night's work are short and dealt with on the same evening and that can be an interview with the law, bollocking from a boss for what he or she sees as you are going too far or sometimes it is the long haul and trust me, the long haul is the sickener.

On an average Saturday night, we are all looking forward to the final bell and a drink afterwards when out of nowhere a Polish guy decides to teach his girl a lesson. He puts a beating on her, and this is a 'no-no'. It wasn't just his fists he used though. No, the scum bag matey had to introduce a bottle into the situation and in one of the nastiest things I've seen on the doors, brought it down on her face. Brought it down good and hard and Jesus, there was blood everywhere.

The poor girl's lip was hanging off the side of her face in a gory, massacre of a mess. She was screaming merry hell, sobbing, and trying to keep her face together. To this day I can still see the horrific picture and only hope it didn't scar her for life, but I bet that it did.

So, any violence is dealt with in our club, but a guy beating a girl, especially with a bottle is a no-brainer.

We reach him and his buddies and our skills are put to the test.

As we throw them out, there is a rumour we gave them a bit of a beating first but us? Nooooo, why would we do something they probably deserved?

As we watch them stagger down the road, we see this as the end of the incident, but these Poles aren't happy and we look on as they go to their van.

In what seems like seconds, they have flung the door to the van open, tooled up and are making their way back toward us, one having the foresight to also use our crowd control barrier against us, picking it up to aim at us.

Now we have been on at the club management for weeks to get the fire-exit bar fixed but would they listen?

So, the loose bar came in handy. As I see my opponent approach, I also so the big 'fuck off' knife in his hand and survival takes over.

It's only one blow to his head but it does the trick

and down he goes.

Unfortunately for both him and me, the blow is a damaging one. He spends the next six weeks in a coma with a bleed on the brain whilst me? Well six weeks, after my arrest, are six weeks of worry. Worry the fucker might die and I'll face a manslaughter charge.

Anyone tells you violence is funny, that it is a game? Remind them of that when the first thing on your mind when you wake up in the morning is that charge hanging over you.

It is the ten years in jail you face, all because some guy decided to teach a lesson to his girl, couldn't accept the lesson he was taught himself by boys bigger than him and decided to arm up.

"You are going away Lee," your inner voice tells you. "You are going away for a long time. Door work? Forget that. Your mates? They will probably have moved on by the time you are out. More than likely married, with a few kids of their own. The Polish guy? Yup, a thuggish idiot but now he will never see the light of day again, so roll back over, close your eyes and try and go to sleep again, okay Lee."

Yes, that is what your inner voice tells you when all they really had to say was "Consequence."

That call though. Man, that call, to say he has woken up and all the mountains on your shoulders are lifted.

But there is still the court date. The barristers, the jury, press the and the police. Your day in court is inevitable, but those two words, those two beautiful words; "Not guilty."

And like that life goes back to normal.

However, readers, I'll answer the question you are asking yourselves. Was I ever really vindicated?

CCTV footage showed the Polish guy attacking me with his blade. It also shows that I hit him only ONCE and that was enough in self-defence.

That same CCTV is now used on S.I.A. training courses when they show bouncers, sorry Door Supervisors what does, and what does not constitute self-defence. Luckily for me it did, and I remained a free man (and rightly so, would say the author Simon Morrell), but the consequence. Damn, that is a big word.

Lessons are learnt though. Mike taught me one of my biggest ones when he showed me you really can fight without fighting and that 'lumping' people isn't always necessary. I was new to the job and green as a freshly mowed lawn. I simply didn't know there was a different way to handle things other than with my fists. Mike knew differently and what I saw him do on this night really affected me.

We have all been in a club or pub when a well-known hard man walks in. Sometimes these guys can be the nicest, most polite, and friendliest people you could meet. Unfortunately, this one wasn't the case.

As door staff, we are aware of the reputations and weight people carry so when these boy walks in we pay extra attention to the matter at hand and sure enough, just minutes after his grand entrance he is on the dance floor throwing hands at people.

Our training kicks in and we make our presence known, but instead of throwing hands back, Mike talks to him nicely and calmly. His demeanour gets the attention of 'ten-men'.

"I need to have a word with you mate," says Mike.

The guy starts to engage in conversation with Mike, but Mike pulls a trick out of his hat.

Squinting against the loud music, he puts his hands to his ear and moves in closer to matey but says, "I can't hear you the bloody music is too loud. Look, let's go upstairs so we can talk properly."

I'm watching on, seeing where this is going and

taking a back seat because I know that Mike really knows his stuff.

We all head up the stairs to the front doors and Mike and matey go outside for their 'chat'.

What Mike did next was so simple it was amazing. He just stepped back inside, shut the door, and left the bloke standing there, speechless.

"Right lads," said Mike. "Back downstairs we still have a night of work on our hands."

It was like being taught by Yoda from Star Wars.

No blood, no missing teeth, no hospital visits, and no arrests. Some might call it poetry from a very wise man.

One of my regrets, later on, is that when I hit the steroids and started getting ripped, my ego became as big as my arms and with it grew my temper. There was simply no backing down from anyone. I didn't care who you were, how massive you might be, if we were doing it, we were doing it; simple.

One night that stands out is the night two bodybuilders decided it was their turn to upset everyone.

My manager saw all this, pretty much everyone in the vicinity was aware of what was going on and so

I was tasked with moving them on, they could be somebody else's problem.

I took the nice approach at first, treating them with respect because that can sometimes do the trick. Not this time though.

"I ain't going anyway mate, fuck off!" was the first one's answer to my request for him to leave.

Anyone in security, whatever level of security that is knows that once your mind is made up and you have given your order, that order must stand. In this game, any change of mind is a backdown, a weakness, and so a 'no-no', but I repeated my request politely.

"Look mate, no need for this. No hard feelings but you must leave for tonight. Always welcome another night," I told him.

As much as my mind was made up, so was his and he repeated his own thoughts.

"I've told you mate, fuck off. We are staying put."

With this, he turned to his mate, and I knew I had to press home my point. 'Talking range' was well and truly over with now so the only answer was to get physical.

I was on the stairs and two steps above him and

given his size, knew any advantage I had I had to take, so leaned down to him and put him in a choke hold but it had no effect, he simply lifted me in the air so I'm now hanging off his back.

'Fight fire with fire.' Anyone who knows anything about fighting will tell you this is one of the ten commandments.

Given his size, I knew I wasn't going to beat him in a square go and so I decided something must give; I chose his eye (and why not, would he have done something equal or worse given his chance?)

I leaned over and push my finger into his eyeball (I'd say the squeamish should look away now, but this poor chap didn't have that luxury).

I'm now up to my first knuckle in slime, gunk and eyeball but this fucker is still protesting and insisting he isn't going anywhere. What? He thought I was going to buy him a drink after this?!

So, in the finger goes, a little bit further and that does the trick. Down he goes, falls to his knees screaming like a stuck pig, and thankfully his mate sees this fight is now over, picks him up and carries him out, luckily giving me time to remove my finger first.

If only he had listened in the first place this could

all have been avoided and he would have been allowed back in another night. Like I say, 'fight fire with fire. Or should that be 'an eye for an eye?'

If I make the doors sound like a constant war ground, an urban battlefield then I am not doing it justice. I met and rubbed shoulders with some famous people including Boxing Heavyweight Champion of the World, Lennox Lewis. Lennox was famous for his two battles with American Evander Holyfield and his war in Cardiff against fellow British man Frank Bruno, but was perhaps best known for beating the baddest man on the planet, 'Iron' Mike Tyson. Lewis systematically took Tyson apart before brutally knocking him out in the eighth round of their battle in Memphis in 2002. I think it is fair to say everyone, including all the door staff was glad he didn't kick off in the Velvet Underground that night.

Other 'faces' that graced us with their presence was Mr Michael 'awight' Barrymore, the singer Lauren Hill, it seemed there was always a famous person in there listening to DJ Carl Cox on a Thursday night (Out? On a school night?). Brandon Block and Alex P were two others who were regulars out as well as the jet set brigade the club also gave way to the newcomers, offering them a chance at their stardom via our showcase nights.

The Velvet Underground would go on to help launch the career of 'the thinking man's Spice Girls' as they showcased the All Saints, one of the most successful bands of the era.

However, one night it was up to my pal and fellow doorman Andy Barclay to spare my blushes when I turned away one of the leading footballers of that time.

Andy was a big Arsenal fan but my knowledge of football was limited to when people would point out a famous player or two. Being caught up in the fight and bodybuilding world, I simply wasn't into the beautiful game and so one night, when I group of guys came up to gain entry to the club, it didn't occur to me that one of them might be a 'name' and so turned them away. Sometimes people don't get entry to a club, it's nothing personal.

The guy told me his name and whom he played for but I wasn't interested. He may as well have been talking double-dutch and so he and his crowd were sent away.

As they made their way down the street, presumably to gain entry elsewhere, Andy came up the stairs and saw who I had knocked back.

Giving me a look that could kill, he ran after them shouting "Come back, come back! We will let you in!'

I had just knocked back one of the country's leading footballers at the time. Nicolas Anelka, he of Arsenal Football Club, the very team my buddy Andy hung his star to and flew their colours

Chapter Seven

When you mention the London night scene to people, they immediately conjure up images of the Kray twins, Jack the Hat, and the Blind Beggar, even though these were a different era altogether.

Now whilst it is true that these boys meant business and that there are certainly people in the Capital City that still know how things 'are done', generally the city center was a fun and safe place to enjoy a night out.

Pills were generally the choice of poison, and they made people really chill.

It wasn't just the punters that enjoyed the details of the illicit stuff. Staff, bosses and others in authority were known to indulge but some more than others and it didn't sit well with certain people.

I didn't really know the boss Tony Tucker, but like every other working man or woman, I sure was glad to see him come Friday nights.

You see that would be the night he would make all the violence, cold nights, and hard work worthwhile when he turned up armed with brown envelopes full of wages. No nicer sight on a freezing Friday in the middle of winter, but like a lot in his business, sometimes that wasn't all he bought.

Standing on the backdoor became my regular place on the team and that is where I found myself on this particular night as Tony, accompanied by another geezer also named Tony (and fellow doorman) told me to turn a blind eye to what they were doing, shut the door and not let anyone onto the fire exit.

I'm just the foot soldier so do as I am told, but a girl who wasn't clued in on the score came over to talk to me. Looking all casual she accidentally leant on the bars of the fire door opening them and showing in all their glory, the two Tonys having a load of gear, but what made the scene even more bizarre is that they were sniffing it from the blade of a fucking big knife that Tony Tucker had on his possession.

I was told very politely to "shut that fucking door!" and so that is what I did. I shut that fucking door sharpish.

So, a week or so goes by and the two are back and it didn't take a genius to work out that they were at it again, only this time, after twenty minutes or so, Tony the doorman comes back in looking all over the place. He just didn't look right or make any sense. And I was naturally a bit concerned.

"Are you okay Tony," I asked him.

He looked at me like he was on the moon and shook his head.

"Nah that cunt Tucker has only gone and given me Ketamine instead of Coke. Fucking hell, mate, he has ruined me."

He staggered off into the club and his own devices, but I later found out the Ket was a lesson taught and a lesson learned.

Tony Doorman had only been dipping into the good stuff of his own accord and behind the boss's back and so Tony Tucker taught the greedy cunt a lesson by switching the marching powder.

Never steal from your own nest, not if you know what is good for you and I guess he was just lucky the boss never bought the knife into play.

Of course, drink makes certain people behave erratically and out of character and this usually leads to violence. In my five nights a week for many years alongside Mike (and others) standing on the city's nightclub doors meant that we would see, stop and break up violence but the real fun, the real eye opener started when I headed home. Yup, it is fair to say that good old Southend on Sea could sometimes feel like a scene from the wild west. Yes, I was home indeed.

My first port of call and door to stand on in sunny Essex was the Sunroom an indy bar with the grunge crowd. It was a great laugh but by far, the thing that stands out about the Sunroom was my introduction to one of the biggest characters I have ever met. Ladies and gentlemen, please be upstanding for Mr Blain Phillips. And please excuse his craziness.

I had met Blain before but now seeing him in action on a regular basis was an education.

Drinking up time is always a tricky one for the door staff. Most will doff their cap good night to you and leave peacefully empty glass or not. Some will acknowledge you and gulp down the last of their hard-earned ale. And then there are the arseholes. Blain did not like arseholes.

This one isn't even subtle. He takes small sip after sip of his drink, and it is like he is trying to antagonise my friend who has a simple solution to the problem.

Reaching into his pocket, he pulls out his cosh and introduces sipper to a headful of pain.

And of course, who can't resist a good throw through the window?

After several smacks around the head, Blain simply picks him up and throws him through the window, shattering the glass and leaving the, by now later drinker, dazed and smashed on the cold concrete.

They fired Blain after that. Bit unfair don't you

think?

Around about the same time I got moved to another club with 'in-house' doormen and so we had the run of the place. I stood one night and saw a lad slap his girlfriend and as said earlier, this is an absolute 'no-no.'

He stormed out of one door as I left via another to meet him.

Being 'the big man' he threatened that I would "get it as well if I didn't move out of the way."

He started to make his move, but I beat him to it by knocking him cold out with a sidekick to the throat.

I watched as he lay on the floor groaning but then he came around, stood up and stared at me, red in the face but with no real clue where he was.

At this time my mate a co door-worker Porky, a big old boy came out, saw this apparent stare out and clock the lad as well.

I suppose the women beater's claim to fame is that he was knocked out twice in one night. Karma comes in many shapes and forms.

So, Southend summer comes to an end and Blain and I find ourselves together again in a place called the Townhouse. It has the inevitable, common problems such as some geezer throwing his weight around and so he has to go, but he goes with the quite usual threat of "yeah, you don't know who you are dealing with. I'll be back to shoot you."

This is something that is heard by every man or girl who has ever stood at the door, and it becomes a kind of white noise.

Except this fucker meant it.

About an hour later we stood around chatting, winding each other up and pushing each other's buttons, same shit different day.

Without any warning, matey is standing in front of us and it is a Mexican standoff. He is staring at us, us at him when the fucker reaches in his jacket, pulls out a gun and fucking shoots at us.

Moving fast? Well, that comes in handy, doesn't it? I jumped one way, Blain the other and the glass behind us to the brunt, taking the bullet for the team.

'Matey' makes his exit, and we say prayers and count our lucky starts. Who says door work is easy money?

Chapter Eight

If I was asked to sum up Blaine, it would be a tricky one but think Austin Powers meets James Bond, but Chopper Reid is the main event.

He was unpredictable to the point his friends gave him the nickname "Reg on the Edge". If that doesn't explain his behaviour then I don't know what will.

His name would not only proceed him but follow him throughout the world.

It is said Blaine didn't look for trouble, he just woke up in the morning and there it was, waiting for him, real handy.

It was certainly waiting for him on his trips to America and even Hawaii where he was asked to leave following his usual antics.

Not the antics that got him thrown off the island but one that springs to mind is when he shot a parrot. Yes, dear reader, you read that right. He shot a parrot. Poor Polly was guilty of nothing more than singing her way through the day, but Blaine didn't like her tune and of course, he shot her. I mean who wouldn't? Shooting a parrot is, to some just another part of the day.

Unfortunately for my good friend, the authorities didn't see it the same way and he was sectioned, spending time in the local nut house before being sent on his way.

However, before he left their fair island he studied local Martial Arts, and in particular Kenpo Karate. His skill levels left everyone impressed and he reached a high level, making a name for himself in local dojos and throughout the island.

Sadly, his mental state and the kind of training he was doing did not go hand in hand.

A good Martial Art, in the hands of a really good Martial Artist is a great thing but when you add a slightly unbalanced mind to that mix, well it has the potential to be a disaster. There were times when he used the skills he had and not in a kind way.

To add to his larger-than-life persona, Blaine also spent time serving in the military, namely the army and as such had access to ammunition and guns. To complete the picture, he had his own Military truck, a big old amphibious thing that he loved to plough through the sea and show off on the roads.

The rifles covering his walls were nothing compared to the love hand grenades that he kept under a box under his bed, and that in itself tells you more about the man. He did not bat an eyelid about sleeping over a box of live bombs. He was a one-man fucking army.

Sadly, his days on the beautiful island were called to a close but not by the authorities. No, he was forced to relocate after a peculiar incident in the toilet of a local bar.

This time Blaine was doing nothing but minding his own business and answering a call to mother nature, of course with a glass of whiskey in his hand.

For reasons unknown or best left unsaid, a local decided to boot the door of the stall in, causing the whiskey glass to shatter in Blaine's face, showering him with the golden liquid.

Blaine being Blaine did not take kindly to this (who would?) and set about teaching the young rascal a lesson, or should I say went to town on him, beating him senseless and leaving him in a pool of his own blood and snot.

Do you know when you are in the wrong place at the wrong time? Well, Blaine was in it.

This guy was no ordinary mug, but a member of the Hawaii Mafia, namely Wilford Pulawa's mob and if there is one thing these organised crime guys hate it is someone busting up one of their own.

Word reached Blaine that he was going to be found,

every one of his limbs chopped off and he would be buried in the Jungle.

Nothing like a bit of motivation to encourage a change of scenery and my friend was on the first plane out.

I can only imagine his sigh of relief as the wheel left the tarmac, but I am also sure it was with sadness as he had to leave all his goods behind. Including his bombs.

Meeting Blaine for the first time was an experience in itself. It was through a mutual friend and when we were all holidaying on the island of Tenerife. At first glance, he came across as a very chilled, long-haired hippie-type dude, but we now know how his looks were deceiving. This guy was anything but chilled.

With the circles I was mixing in at this time, it was no surprise to me that we were staying in the apartment of a very well-connected underworld figure, Mr John Palmer, who later was murdered, no doubt due to his role and part in the said underworld.

So, whilst it was no surprise to be in such a character's apartment.

One of our guys was busy doing his business in the

apartment's toilets and after a session on the beer, I was desperate for a wee. Ten minutes is a long time holding a bladder full of ale and after waiting as long as I could, mother nature won the battle of wills.

The result was my waste was air-bound over the balcony from about six floors up, making a less-than-graceful landing on the pool area below.

Mr Palmer got word of this and the next day I was given a stern talking too.

But boys will be boys and things started getting out of hand even though I was given instructions to calm myself down.

Apparently, we were surrounded by the cream of the underworld. The last thing these 'names' wanted was to watch a group of lads behaving like a gang on an 18-30's stag do, but on a belly full of ale and a few lines, I've decided am not taking crap off anyone.

"My holiday, my rules," was what must have been going through my mind as I issued the warning that "I'm not scared of anyone, I'll fight whoever."

However, my warning came from something like a Crocodile Dundee movie as a blade as big as I had ever seen (and I have seen many) was produced a stuck into the table. It was so big it wobbled like a bowl of jelly, weird wobbly sounds coming from the vibrating steel.

"We don't do fights out here son," growled an aggressive southern voice to me. "You'll end up being gutted, a knife just like this one here being stuck in you."

Now I listened to the warning but I'm not sure I took it seriously as the next day I found myself in the local diving shop, browsing for my own steel.

I found one that would match theirs' and of course, the seller didn't ask any questions, he was just grateful for my coin.

I wasn't taking any chances, if they were going to try and use me as a dart board me and my sharp buddy would make sure they worked for it.

Luckily the rest of the shenanigans passed without incident, and I remained puncture free, but that blade never left my side until I was safely homebound.

Chapter Nine

As much as I loved doing the doors, the pay wasn't enough and I was certainly done with poverty, so it was time to supplement my income and so took up a driving job. Unwittingly it put me in a place as dangerous as even door work was.

Higgs International seemed like a good fit for my new career. They supplied newspapers all over Europe, long before the days of e-prints and the like of.

My job was to cross the channel and get the papers such as The Sun and The Mirror to the British holidaymakers and ex-pats that formed the communities on the other side of the water.

The chariot that awaited me had 'press' written on the side of it, just like all the other vans and lorries making that same trip which made us very popular with the guards and customs on both sides of the channel. We would give the French guys copies of the English red tops and o the return journey, their English colleagues the French versions of the same and so they would see us and wave us through. Getting stopped was rare so it was inevitable what would happen in the future; smuggling.

My ticket (no pun intended) was through a character in the Essex underworld, who as luck would have it had a business in Brussels that made 'car parts'. You tell me?

Didn't matter though as it was a great way to get his cocaine into Britain, and then move it around the country from there.

Our usual haul was one thousand pounds to bring back a kilo of coke and so the reward outweighed the risk, especially as we wouldn't put the coke inside the wagons just in case we were pulled.

Instead, we worked out a plan that seemed foolproof but even that could send your heart into overdrive.

The guys at the port had an x-ray machine that was basically a long metal tunnel that could see through everything. If you hid coke in your tires you were done for, if you took a chance and removed a panel to hide the coke behind, tough shit, you are caught. Anywhere inside the vehicle was fair game but we soon realised that we, mere humans weren't.

There was no way we could stay in the van as it made the short journey through the tunnel to get scanned, so we had to walk the distance and meet it on the other side, the exit to the tunnel to avoid the radiation from the machines. And guess what? No scans for us.

And so, when I was approached and offered a thousand pounds a kilo I jumped at the chance. Now multiply that by four. Four thousand pounds to wear a pair of women's tights and pack the coke to my body, only then wearing a baggy tracksuit over to conceal my haul.

Looking back, I realise that I had been foolish, if I had been caught it is up to ten years inside but remember I grew up poor, I grew up in massive poverty without a pot to piss in, so he without sin can throw the first stone. If you are poor and somebody waves a grand in front of you, chances are you are going to take it and that is what I did.

That chance involved meeting a complete stranger at an unmanned petrol station somewhere near the border, strapping up the drugs and taking the biggest chance of my life, only being able to breathe properly again when I was back on Blighty soil and my cash in my hand.

When I think about it now, I wondered how I ever got involved in such capers, but the truth is it was quite a simple move from driver to international drug smuggler and as usual in these matters, it came down to who, not what, you know.

I had a friend in the Essex underworld (as you do)

and he knew I was now doing regular runs to France with the British papers.

He approached me with the famous last words, "Do you want to earn yourself some extra money?" and of course, my answer was yes.

Without another thought, we sat in the inevitable pub to meet a guy who looked like the character Bricktop from Guy Ritchie's movie 'Snatch'. An old boy, with grey hair, and glasses, the geezer even spoke like him.

So, the meeting begins and old Bricktop proceeds to tell me how things work and how he runs a car business in Belgium but again, you tell me. Did he?

After the deal was explained to me and I agreed on terms, the geezer starts to wipe down all the glasses as if to remove any trace of him being there.

Turns out he was paranoid that he was being watched, and sadly for him his paranoia proved right. He must have been under police surveillance because later he was nicked and ended up doing ten years inside. The price you pay, I guess.

My own time to pay was on its way as well and as I came through to the ferry, it became obvious they searched us differently to the Channel Tunnel. As I went into customs on the way home, I was pulled over by the boys in uniform.

At this time, I was bringing I tobacco to sell, but by now the temptation of the money was proving greater than any fear of consequence I had.

As well as looking at every nook and cranny, inside the wheels, behind and under the seats, even in the exhaust pipe, these boys were determined to find something on me and insisted that I had a false floor built into the bed of the truck. So, for the next four hours, I waited, sweating nervously as they dismantled my vehicle.

In the end, they settled their focus on the fact I had two different brands of cigarettes and whilst I could have unlimited amounts for my own consumption, they simply didn't buy into my story.

I tried to convince them that the reason I had so much volume of the two brands was that my trips were not frequent and so I took advantage of this rare outing abroad to stock up on smokes for my missus and me.

Nope, they weren't buying it but all through our negotiations, they failed to notice my sweating forehead and slightly shaking hands. The reason for this? I was strapped up with coke and they never suspected it for one minute.

Even though I was shitting myself I continued to argue my case because who wouldn't if they were just over the limit on tobacco?

To this day I can never understand why they just didn't pat me down because they must have known I was up to something by my very demeanour. Was someone up there looking out for me?

So empty-handed of cigarettes but chock full of cocaine, I made my way home with a little laugh and looked forward to cashing in. Happy days!

Not everything went as smoothly as this though and I found myself at the end of another risk versus reward situation.

During one trip to Calais to do our business, one of the guards set up an ambush with our agreement. He would double our money if, as we handed over the goods, we would play our part in a guy coming up behind us on a motorbike, 'bashing' us over the head (with minimum force) and then the plan was for him to rob us both of drugs and money and riding off into the sunset like a hero in a cowboy film.

Meanwhile, we and the guy we are doing business with are left with nothing to show for it and we can't be held accountable to our bosses as we were the victims here.

Other than a superficial sore head there is no harm done, but we settle up on the quiet later on.

Except the clown on the bike hadn't read up on 'reasonable force' and properly did me in.

Instead of pulling his blow, I felt the full force of his cosh and so any playacting on my part to look dazed, for anyone watching on was totally unnecessary as the headache, seeing stars and stumbling about were all totally real. No need for role play, just a cracking headache for days and another lesson learnt

Chapter Ten

The thing with long-distance lorry driving, whether delivering newspapers or dropping off bags of coke, is that it gives you time to think. There are only so many songs on the radio you can listen to, only so many news programs and so you think and that thinking inevitably leads to reminiscing. It takes you back in time and on those long stretches of the motorway I started to think back to my dad. A dad I didn't know for a long time and when I did, he was cruelly snatched away.

My first memory of him as a young nipper was when we visited our dear old nan, who was my dad's mum. I loved my nan and saw her a lot, but it wasn't until I was about eight that I went to visit her one day only to be greeted by the sight of my father sitting in the kitchen. Ironically enough, despite all the harsh words my mother had to say about him, it was she who inadvertently made that first introduction. Whatever my mum was, she never denied my nan the chance to see her grandkids, hence why we were regular visitors so I suppose it was always on the cards that we would bump into him, accidentally or otherwise.

My nan made the introductions, father to son and she was delighted we had finally met. It would seem so was my dad as he gave me a massive cuddle, the first time I had felt my father's arms around me.

As we cuddled, mum and my nan sat down to a cup of tea and then he suddenly stood up and announced he was going training.

And so off we went the two of us to a home-made weights gym in my nan's garage. I was thrilled that he had asked me to go and set about, in my juvenile mind 'proving myself to him by lifting very light weights. I loved it, a lad and his dad training together although I wasn't sure exactly what training was.

My delight grew as we saw more of each other, and he asked me to go and stay with him. I was so excited to go and again took the trip to my nans' house in preparation to visit my dad's house.

To this day I have no clue what happened to stop the visit. All I knew was that my nan told me I couldn't go and stay with him and, seeing I was upset exchanged his cuddles for her and told me to stay with her.

I ended up not staying with her that night and instead, being totally pissed off made the journey back home and another night surrounded by skinheads and party animals. My childhood seemed to be slipping away too fast.

It would be a while before I saw my dad again and even that was under upsetting circumstances.

Mum, ever one to hold a grudge and spite her son, set me up to fail and her set-up worked well.

She found out where my dad now lived and, aware he had a new woman in his life along with the two small children he had with her (my stepbrothers, only babies really), my mum nudged me in the right direction.

"Here you are son," she offered, all smiles and sunlight. "This is where your dad lives now. Go on son, go and see him, it will make up for the lost time. Just knock on the door and say hello. He'll be delighted to see you."

So. I am just a kid right, and I believe my mum, I believe her because I want to believe her.

I tell myself, "Yes! I get to see my dad and he will be so pleased to see me! What a great surprise!"

With my heart bursting and a stomach full of butterflies, I knocked on the door and it was opened by a kid of about fifteen, slightly older than me.

His confused look at seeing me didn't deter me.

"Hello," I said to him. "Is my dad here please?"

So. the kid's confusion grows at this, but he shuffles away and I can hear the muted conversation between him and somebody else inside the house.

It isn't my dad that comes to greet me but a young woman who turned out to be my dad's new wife.

Her confusion matched the young kid's when she asked what I wanted, and I told her I was looking for my dad.

She wandered off back into the house and then lo and behold there he was, my father, standing right in front of me. His attention was split between me, his fist born son at his front door, and the muttering between him and his wife.

Her muttering didn't last long as she lost her cool during the muted argument and she started shouting at him. Without any further words to me, she slammed the door leaving me standing alone in the street.

Gutted, I did the only thing a young boy can do in this type of circumstance and just walked away. As I made my way through the park and back to my cousin's house it occurred to me that he might not have even told her about me and so her shock was probably as big as my disappointment.

If I thought I was upset at my dad slamming the

door, what greeted me when I got home was even worse. My mum was delighted.

"Yeah!" she shouts laughing as she greets me. "He doesn't want to know you, I didn't expect anything else!"

Somewhere between my father's shock and my mother's delight was a heartbroken young boy and it would be a long time until I would speak to him again.

It seems as I shift through the gears of the truck, I shift through the gears of my childhood and suddenly, I'm not that kid anymore but an eighteen-year-old on the brink of manhood, all with a twenty-eight-year-old girl at my side.

To escape the clutches of my mum, who tried to run my life, monitoring my every move being the control freak she was and after an argument that is that long ago now, I can't even remember what it was about, I packed my bags and moved in with my new girl.

This drove my mum to new levels of hate and manipulation, and she started calling the girl up, throwing all sorts of spanners in the works, at one point suggesting she kicks me out because I was cheating on her.

Then she upped the game again when there was a pregnancy scare and we thought a bay was on the way. My mum flew into a fury, perhaps this little one was another person to steal her limelight who knows but her behaviour upon hearing of the possible birth was outrageous.

"If she has that baby," she ranted "I'll kill it. That baby is as good as dead."

As it happens, there was no baby and so everybody was spared an absolutely horrific gesture, but it didn't stop my mum continue to try and control me as I continue to cosy up to the girl, enjoying my life, enjoying my independence.

Then in a completely bizarre act and change of allegiance, my mum phones my dad for help. She paints him a wicked picture of my girl, calling her a wrong 'un and telling my dad he needs to get to my new place and get me out of there.

"This tart is going to turn him bad," would be the sort of vocabulary she would use.

I'm eighteen now and I've seen and been through so much I am my own man. I am a fighter both in the streets and the controlled arena so when my mum tells me my dad is coming around, I shrug my shoulders.

"So what? I am not listening to him. After all, you have said about him, you think I'll take any notice of the man?" That was my reaction and answer to my mother's threats.

Yeah right. 'Wait 'til your father gets home.'

He makes his grand entrance and now I realise she had filled him with the same poison that she had endured upon me.

He starts to give me his fatherly advice and how the girl is no good for me, I need to get out and how he only wants the best for me.

Years and years of hurt, neglect and mistreatment all came out at once as I stomped my 'alpha-male' foot down.

I reared at him, told him in no uncertain terms that he had no rights over me, he wasn't there when I needed him so how dare he try and be now?

We butted horns, two stags pushing each other in a field and his alpha male showed its face too as he threatened to take me "around the back to give me a good hiding."

Now my life is fighting, and I am past giving one

fuck for anyone, so the challenge is accepted. I threw my coat to the floor and called him it.

"Okay, let's go!" I told him.

With his bluff called he backed down and try to take back his threats, saying that wasn't what he meant but the damage was done.

"Fuck off," I told him.

Fuck off he did, and he would stay fucked off for many years to come. He only came back into my life when I had one of the greatest gifts a man could have; children of my own.

My dad swallowed whatever pride men have when it comes to falling out with their own sons and he made contact as he wanted to see Crystal, my daughter.

It was a soul-searching moment and kind of heart-breaking to decide to let him back into my life. Soul searching because I wanted to give him the benefit of the doubt and let Crystal have a granddad, but heart-breaking because I couldn't quite connect the dots.

"How come he wants to see his granddaughter but never wanted to see me?" I was forced to ask myself.

The thing is, once our masks had slipped and we were almost forced to be civil to one another, he was a really nice man. Never turned up at my home empty-handed. Always bought clothes and gifts for the kids and forever plonked down a bag of shopping on the family table as he came in.

The wounds healed quickly and I was now a regular visitor at his house for a Sunday roast, our relationship being mended over a table of hot food, a room of good chat and the cuddles I missed out on as a kid. I came to love both these cuddles and my dad.

Those Sundays extended themselves to a first Christmas together, which went on to become a second, all to the dismay of my bitter mother who hated it all.

I could live with that, I loved my dad and realised I had missed him growing up more than I thought.

Fate can be beautiful reuniting a father and son, but faith can also be the biggest bitch you will ever meet, and I met the latter when I received a phone call that bought me such terrible news and heartache.

My dad discovered he had motor neuron disease and had probably less than three months to live. Smack me around the head with a cosh on a dodgy drug deal in France over that news any day. That pain you physically feel, that smack on the head is tangible, but this news? Fuck that.

My mum took the news as I expected my mum to take the news; with spite.

"He is full of sit that one," she told me. "Always seeking attention. Don't listen to him son, there is fuck all wrong with him."

I must have been in denial as I initially agreed with her, on some level anyway.

Her theory seemed to stand up when I saw my dad sitting down with no neck brace on, only moving to wear it when I entered the room as he stood to greet me and so I felt justified in doubting him. It was only when I realised that he was putting it on so he had more movement did I grasp the truth of the matter. He was indeed poorly

Some people say they have the 'king of hangovers', but the one I had on a Sunday morning after a night on the doors and a few drinks, was only partly the fault of the beer.

I was lying in bed feeling as rough as the bottom of a birdcage and not bothering with my phone. Trying to sleep away the booze, I eventually relented and saw that I had a ton of missed calls. My nan and my cousin Danielle had been trying to reach me with the same message.

"Lee, your dad is dying. You need to get up to the hospice as soon as you can. Your dad is asking for you."

It remains the biggest regret of my life that I didn't make it.

My dad died on that Sunday afternoon in Haven's Hospice.

When people pass away, we look for the good in them and we usually find moments that mean a lot and stay with us forever.

When I was a baby, my dad's dad, my grandad was a wrestler and a well known street fighter. He looked at me and told my dad "This boy is going to be a fighter son."

He was right and I am very proud that my dad could at least see me being awarded my black belt and a couple of my cage fights. And that, as they say, is my old man in a nutshell.

Chapter Eleven

My truck is travelling along just nicely, bobbing along France's A2 heading for a drop at Saint-Denis. As I reach down for my cup of tea from the flask, I catch sight of a group of caravans parked at the side of the road and instantly realise they are travellers, also grabbing their refreshments on the journey down the road.

They make me smile as it brings back another memory, another character, another fucking nutter; Craig Wallace.

There is an old joke that goes something like this; "Why do travellers complain when they are asked to move on?"

You would hope when you told this joke to Craig you would catch him on a good day, for he was a ferocious fighter when angered.

Short and stocky with the traveller's trademark ginger hair, from the first night on the door together there was a mutual dislike. That would change later on, but those first few times together were frosty to say the least.

As we stood keeping guard of the door, he would be immersed in his bodybuilding magazines, chewing the arse out of me by telling me what protein he had taken that day, and what the latest and greatest supplements were, whilst I would roll my eyes, groan inwardly and say to myself, "not another one of them."

On the other hand, he would think I was moody and arrogant as I didn't engage in many conversations with him.

Despite all this, it turned out we part of the same crowd. Knowing the same people, and the same faces saying hello can be an ice breaker, and on a night out, and the inevitable few beers we started chatting and found out we got on really well. A friendship would be formed out of what was first, hostility toward each other.

It isn't a night out on the ale unless it finishes at the burger van and this night would prove to be no different, but as always, where males gather when they are full of drink, violence is never far behind.

It kicked off and we were 'all in' when I saw for the first time, someone being taken to the floor and that someone was Craig.

As he was fighting from his back, I remained upright and was throwing punches with all I could muster at the lemon in front of me. After all, he was throwing punches at me so it would be rude not to return the favour.

Our combatives were interrupted by a scream that I can only describe as a pig being stuck.

Turning and expecting to see Craig in deep waters, I was instead greeted with the site of flesh flying through the air and this was the source of the screaming.

Craig had pulled the guy in close which is quite a typical move when you are fighting from your back. What he did next wasn't so typical.

He pulled the guy in so close that he was in biting range, and this was where Craig took the fight and a piece of the guy's cheek. Dinking his teeth in, ripping the flesh, and spitting it out may be all very primal, but isn't that what fighting is?

What was even more primal was when he went back for his pudding, his desserts as his teeth found flesh and a massive chink of his opponent's teeth followed through the air. One way of topping up your protein shakes I suppose.

The thing is, once you have broken the ice with a

man and then find yourselves fighting on the same side, you create a bond. Craig and I got on really well and became good drinking buddies, so much so that he started to socialise in my circles, with my friends.

So, as well as his own crowd his now mixing with us, Gary Gordon, Porky, Simon Wilkinson, all good friends, all guys who have your back. In return, I am introduced to some big names in his community, travellers in their own underworld and it quickly becomes a thing, a circle in itself. But of course, trouble loves company and we seemed to always find ourselves in the thick of it.

An ordinary party on an ordinary weekend night soon becomes an event in itself.

On pretty much every occasion where there is booze and males, no matter where you are in the world, there is always someone who fancies himself to be the alpha male. This party was no different.

Making myself at home, I took a seat and settled down to enjoy the festivities, when I hear a growl from behind me.

"Oi!" is how I am addressed. "Get out of that chair. That's the King's chair."

Now I look down and I don't see a throne, just an

ordinary living room seat, but it is this man's house and politeness can go a long way, so I oblige and give up the chair.

He grunts at me as he takes his seat and I take his grunt as his way of saying thank you.

Truth be told, this guy, surrounded by his girls, drugs and hoodlums thinks he is something special, but we have seen better men.

Craig watches this exchange from the side-line and gives me the nod, it is a nod to say, "I've got you."

I return the nod and then mayhem erupts.

Craig jumps up, pulls out a fuck off blade and screams at the guy, "Give me all your drugs!"

"Well, that escalated quickly," I thought to myself as the King tells Craig to "fuck off!"

Craig won't have any of it but thankfully, instead of using his blade he just clumps the guy, smashing him in the face.

Now this man can it hard at the best of times but now I realise he is wearing a knuckle duster and the damage these can do is horrendous.

So now we cotton on that the guy must be a dealer because he screams at his girls, through clots of blood and broken teeth, to get us what we ask for and they have obliged by throwing huge amounts of drugs at us.

Craig is still not happy and demands more and his request is obliged, but now we come to realise we have put another mate in a terrible position.

People are screaming at Gary to tell him to get his mates (us) under control and in turn, Gary is screaming at me and Craig to stop.

Little ginger Craig will have none of this, this is his raid, and the spoils are his, so he tells Gary to fuck off.

"You can have some as well if you want," he screams. "I'll fucking cut you open!"

Gary knows a serious man when he sees one and he saw one in Craig on this night. He does the right thing, he steps away and amazingly, we all leave together, but Gary is not a happy man, in fact far from it. He is incredibly pissed off at us.

He tries to read us the riot act, but his force is met with a stronger one in Craig, who repeats his desire to cut Gary if Gary doesn't "shut the fuck up!"

Gary does just that, shuts the fuck up but to this day he has not forgotten and although we are all still mates, brings it up whenever he gets the opportunity and uses it against us when we piss him off. Still a bloody good friend though, him and Craig.

Not sure if the King still sits on his throne but there was so much blood from him that night t would cost a pretty penny to dry clean.

The thing is with Craig, adventures were never far away, and his looks could be deceiving. Because of his lack of height and body language he didn't really look like much to be reckoned with. That is until you were stupid enough to try and believe me, people tried.

After a night on the booze at the popular Baker's Bar, we found ourselves in the usual position of queuing for the inevitable burger to help soak up the alcohol.

Of course, we weren't the only ones with the munchies, but some thought their hunger to be more important than ours and decided to jump the line of waiting pundits, much like t.v presenters at a state funeral.

Craig never did care much for the Philips and Hollies of this world and was very straightforward with his words, letting them know in no uncertain terms that what he was suggesting wasn't a request, but more a direct order.

"Oi!" he shouts. "Get back in the fucking queue like the rest of us! No jumping the line."

The reply he received was never going to calm the matter and the inevitable was, well inevitable.

"Fuck off little man," says the queue jumper and that was all it took.

Craig didn't carry a knuckle duster as in one of them. No, Craig always went for overkill and so produced and proceeded to fit onto his large hands, not one but two dusters.

After cracking the guy to teach him a lesson, we heard the ever-familiar sound of police sirens, as plod rushed to the scene to deal with the matter.

We weren't going to hang around and so without further ado, we took to our feet, running from the scene and escaping any punishment.

Problem is, nice we were out of sight, out of mind we realise we had forgotten a very important thing; we didn't get our food and were fucking starving!

Tots was one of the area's leading night spots and one that came under my guard, and that was what I was doing on this particular night, guarding the door when who should turn up? The Ginger Ninja himself, Craig Wills.

As much as I loved the guy sometimes my heart would sink at the sight of him strolling toward the door.

"Ahh please don't start anything tonight, Craig," I would think. Sometimes even the best of doormen could do with an easy night.

All is well to start with and Craig goes inside and boozes his night away, but the patron Saint of doorstaff often takes the piss out of his and creates his own mischief and yup, this was one of those nights.

As I am throwing a yahoo out of the club for some misdemeanour or other, Craig makes an appearance, coming outside for a smoke.

He watches the action, seemingly an innocent bystander but then revs the punter up.

"Did you hear that mate?" he asks him. "Fuck me, they just called you a weasel."

As he was just out of our earshot, we had no idea what was said until said weasel approach us.

"What the fuck did you call me? A fucking weasel?"

As I saw Craig laughing in the background, I quickly worked out what had happened and really couldn't be arsed about getting into nonsense with this guy so tried to cool it all down. Not a chance.

"Nah, fuck 'em mate!" shouts Craig to the guy. "They just threw me out as well! For no fucking reason!" He even managed to sound indignant and his new best friend believed him, making his own war cries.

"Let's team up and do 'em!" shouts Craig and matey agrees, but as he moves toward us full of menace and bravado now he is backed up, Craig 'switches teams' and smashes him in the side of the face.

The poor guy, stunned, hits the floor whilst trying to look at Craig with hurt feelings at the betrayal.

Craig just nods at him, lights up another ciggie and tells him, "He is right you know, you are a fucking weasel."

The thing with working the doors is that it has the lot. Tears, laughter, violence, love and of course its fair share of black humour. The thing that you can't help but laugh at even though the situation may be a dangerous, possibly deadly one.

And so, this was the situation I and my fellow door staff found ourselves in one night as we stood at the door of a club, appropriately named 'Mayhem.' Should have seen the omens.

The club was the next best thing, the place everybody wanted to be seen in. An all-singing, all-dancing, modern den of inequity.

On this particular evening, we had had some trouble with a bunch of black guys, who seemed hell-bent on trouble. They had to be dealt with appropriately and that meant showing them the door. We dealt with these guys in the same way we would deal with a group causing bother, but like anybody who gets thrown out, they got the hump with us. To say they were not happy would be, well an understatement.

They made the same noises, the same threats that probably every doorman and woman throughout the land and all through time has heard; "We will be back to shoot you." They went one step further by using some American vocabulary;' "We are going to bust a cap in your ass."

Now the thing is, the majority of people issuing these threats do so as they walk in the opposite direction as to where those threats should actually take place, and that is away from us.

Not this crew though. Within thirty minutes they had returned and positioned themselves directly opposite the entrance to Mayhem, where they proceeded to eye-fuck us, bad intentions quite evident.

As our Mexican standoff took place, we heard over the club radio system the words we were dreading.

"He's got a gun!"

Fuck me, I have never seen some guys run so fast, as they bolted from their place on the door, leaving only the brave behind.

After all, where else could we go? The main entrance had to remain open as we still had punters coming in and out and so the stare-out competition continued, but now we are aware they appear to have come good on their threats to shoot us and have indeed returned armed up.

Our manager ran to the office to call the police as we waited for the inevitable.

Thank God it never came. As we all stood staring, nobody knowing quite what to do, it started to become apparent what we had heard and it was nothing but the bar staff relaying over the radio that what we knew as a zapper or scanner for the bar codes on the drinks, they called a gun and that someone's had broken, but somebody else had a replacement 'gun.'

Relief flooded through us as even the hardiest amongst us likes to get home without being shot…or scanned and charged £2.75 for it.

We seem to spend our time between the gym, the clubs and of course the parties, and there is no party like a Basildon party, so that is where we found ourselves in the early hours of this particular morning.

Craig had been 'on it' and had a case of the paranoias. There was a gaggle in the kitchen and he got it into his head they were talking about him, taking the piss.

Now I don't know if that was exactly true but they were certainly up to something and so I watched it start to unfold.

"What the fuck are you saying about me?" he slurred and without warning, reared up, pulled out his Stanley Knife and slashed two of these guys.

Whilst they weren't deep cuts, they were enough to send claret around the room and a sense of sock and alarm amongst the revellers.

The guys that were cut may have had good reason, but they did something you don't do in our circles; they went to the police.

And that is how Craig found himself in the unfortunate position of having the leave the country. If he was caught, arrested and charged, they aren't going to give a character like him community service and so he got on his toes.

Australia was his choice of destination and it seemed it would be the making of him. He and I stayed in touch regularly and he would tell me how he was staying out of trouble, had turned over a leaf and so forth, but it wouldn't last.

In true Craig fashion, he found himself on the wrong side of the law again.

Again, blades were involved, as were two guys and after opening them up, my old friend found himself in an Australian jail.

Upon his release, his time in the sun was over and the authorities deported him and so my ginger mate found himself back on Blighty soil, rain and clouds and all.

It seems like trouble got on the flight back home with him because it was just a matter of time before the law involved itself in his life again.

This time he was arrested by two police officers for some affray or another and they tried to cuff him. He would have nine of and as they tried to apply a 'Home Office Approved Technique' and twist his arms up his back, he exploded and lay the two out.

A day in Court was now inevitable but this time luck shone on my buddy.

He had a good solicitor, an even better barrister and they managed to get the case thrown out. Despite the CCTV showing the event happened exactly as the officers of the law said, they lied about their rank, claiming they were the police when in fact they were only PCSOs (Police Community Support Officers). They must not have had the same powers of arrest and who knows, on the night in question, with overinflated egos and quite possibly acted above their actual powers.

The Ginger Ninja, Craig Wills walked out of that court a free man and into a new life.

The fighting traveller, troublemaker extraordinaire, drinker, smoker and a good solid friend walked away from it all, turned his life around and has never been in trouble since. Now a family man, he keeps his nose clean and his hands honest; having kids will do that to you, won't it?

Chapter Twelve

Vale Tudo; What the cool kids now call Cage Fighting.

Fighting is in your blood. It is certainly in mine and has been since day one. Some people get their first smack whether it be in the controlled arena or a go in the street, but that first smack defines them.

Some give their head a shake and walk away, avoiding any conflict for the rest of their lives and never stepping foot in a Combat Academy.

And then there is us. The people who love it, can't get enough of a good ruck or a five-rounder in a local sports hall on a Saturday night.

Doesn't make us any better. It just makes us different. I wouldn't have it any other way.

I had already established myself as a Karate man, a Kickboxer and a street fighter when UFC came along. I became absorbed in it, watching the Gracies, the crazy fighting family from Brazil who, it is said led a balanced life between MMA and gangster hood. Didn't matter to me, the two can and sometimes do go hand in hand so it was all the same to see them do their thing in the cage.

Then there was Ken Shamrock, an American

Wrestler who made the transition into MMA look easy, becoming a legend in both disciplines.

So, I mentioned to Steve 'Nipper' Ellis that I had been watching all of this and with my stuff, the Thai boxing, Judo etc I told him this is where I wanted to be, in the cage.

It was music to my ears when Steve told me that he knew someone who did all this and that he would make the connection, hook me up with the guy.

Said guy was a gentleman called Daniel Burzotta who invited me to train with him in his garage.

What we trained in was actually called Vale Tudo which had its origins, believe it or not, in the circuses of Brazil.

Whilst the history of it all was interesting, I just wanted to get stuck in and what better man to start me on this next path

than Daniel?

He had already travelled across the pond to America to train with the Royce Gracie and was a member of the English Ju-Jitsu team, the Japanese style of it.

As well as holding both European and World medals, he was also a Black belt in Ju-Jitsu and Judo and if you add his Kickboxing skills to an already very impressive arsenal, you had a great all-round fighter.

To say training with Dan and training in a range so alien to me was an eye-opener would be a massive understatement.

I quickly realised my time in Judo had been spent mostly learning holds and I quickly felt limited in this range.

Despite this feeling, I absolutely loved it even though I felt like a piece of rope being tied up in knots.

I was taken to pieces with arm bars, leg triangles, you name it Daniel put it on me, but I didn't complain, just kept getting up for more, thinking "let's go again!"

Luckily for me, as Dan grew so did I. I was with him when he opened his own club and started to attract students, the kind you want to be on the mats with. Guys who would train hard, the type that wouldn't cry off if they got hurt, no broken nails or fragile egos allowed.

2005 came along and with it my first ever MMA fight and it was a guy that would go on to become four times World Kickboxing Champion, Mr Andrew 'Cobra' Tate. Andrew is also a self-made millionaire, a huge success outside of the fighting arena with his own YouTube chat show and a range of high-sports cars at his beck and call.

I was to learn a very hard lesson as I trained and took part in this first MMA fight and I broke every rule in the fighter's book; I didn't take it seriously. Any young bucks out there reading this and hoping to embark on their own fight journey, what I am about to tell you is not how you prepare for any fight.

My life was working the doors, partying, drinking more than my fair share of booze and neglecting my training. Not altogether, I was still at it on the mats but not with the kind of commitment needed for a fight of this calibre.

I was cocky and too confident, and I thought this would just be a fight like any other, a Karate tournament, a low-level Kickboxing bout but boy was I wrong.

I even ignored Daniel's pleas for me to train harder, instead listening to my own voice that told me I knew best, I knew better.

Strangely enough, in the first round, I breezed it. Absolutely smashed it, but when the time came for round two, I was gone. You could find whatever was left of my breathing sitting in the back row, watching the fight whilst eating popcorn. I had gassed and had nothing left in my tank.

It was like watching myself on film getting hit, taking the punches seemed much easier than actually fighting back.

Even my poor diet had a pop at me as I came in over the weight limit which meant to cut that weight, I had to spend the morning in a sauna and then on the exercise bike, all in an effort to shift the excess three kilos that my lifestyle had presented me with. I simply had nothing left to give.

In a final push to salvage the fight I shot for a double leg takedown, but Andrew simply put me in a single-arm choke to which I had no choice but to tap. No excuses, no looking around for someone to blame, this was me. This was all me.

Andrew went on to achieve great things and I'll take nothing away from him, but whilst he was training hard, I was boozing. I honestly think if I had have made better choices, the outcome would have been a different one. We live and learn.

I'm not a quitter. For all that life has thrown at me I will not throw in the towel and so picking myself up from the defeat, I hit the gym running and there is no pun intended in any of that sentence.

I threw the lot in, determined to do better and by the time I faced the Mexican Fernando Saucier, I was at my peak condition. Poor Fernando bore the brunt of my previous loss as I took it to him, the fight lasting a grand total of 24 seconds. I had appeased myself, done myself proud.

This type of fighting would thankfully spill over into another very important part of my life; the door.

Now I know how to choke someone into submission, I no longer need to orbit them into space with a right hook to the jaw. All very pleasant viewing for the ever-present CCTC cameras, that monitored our every move, providing the police, the CPS and our glorious court system with all they need to know to put us away.

No, gone are the days of clumping people. Now it is just easier to put the anaesthetic on them by way of cutting off the blood supply to the brain.

It also very conveniently does away with any cuts, bruises or abrasions. I mean when was the last time you went to sleep and woke up looking like a bruised peach? No, those days were over.

The ability to move someone from inside the club to outside the club for acting like a complete dick was also a lot easier using an arm or shoulder lock.

Covering our backs from any legal eagles was always a big factor in this game and so learning BBJ was a real asset to me.

And then there was Porky. Man, what a character. Porky and I worked the doors together and he introduced me to people like Greenie which meant we found ourselves growing as a pack.

As with every pack we were loyal to each other and that loyalty was reinforced by training together at Jim Connor's Progress House, another very well-known bodybuilder's gym. As well as being known for its first-rate training, it was also widely known by those who needed to know that this was the place to go for steroids and this is what we wanted. We wanted to bulk up and put more armour on our bodies for the various activities and ventures we had, including the door work and competing. It seemed the two went hand in hand.

Progress House was also the place where I first met Steve 'Nipper' Ellis, another guy who would become a big feature in my life.

My first impressions of Nipper were not exactly ones that would make us the good friends we later became.

People knew of his reputation, knew he was a capable man and as such 'kissed his arse' and that just wasn't me.

Nipper though, well he would take one look at these suck-ups and know exactly what they were about. This meant he would take liberties and be rude and abrasive knowing they would laugh it off, embarrassed but unable to do anything about it.

There were lots of stories floating about saying he had held people at gunpoint, but it quickly became apparent these stories were bullshit.

It was just another part of folklore, tales told by people who thought this was some sort of fucking Western film and they had a lead part.

As for Nipper, deep down he hated bullies and would put people to the test with his cutting words.

And here, strangely enough, is where our friendship was born. I didn't really give a fuck for anyone and would either answer him back or choose to ignore him completely.

This piqued Nipper's interest, got his respect and we started to become buddies.

We would start seeing each other out at the same clubs and Nipper being Nipper, would always know where the after-party was. It wasn't long before I was invited along as his guest.

Sadly, I our friendship grew so did his paranoia and in one incident, he found a gun in my room.

He became convinced I was out to get him on behalf of the Essex Boys and it took a while for him to believe me when I told him I wasn't.

Why didn't I just walk away? Well, I knew that the base of his paranoia, the root problems lay with his old friend Pat Tate.

Tate tried to kill Nipper over a stupid remark he made to Tony Tucker's girlfriend when she phoned him to ask where Tony was.

"Probably at home fucking the arse off his missus," was his reply, but that kind of talk did not go down well in these circles.

These were volatile people, quick to be offended and even quicker to seek retribution.

Tony would take the falling out to the heart and went to the extremes banging a gun against is head before throwing him to the bed and threatening to cut his arm off with a hatchet .

The final straw in this matter was when Tucker threatened to kidnap Nipper's younger sister and hold her hostage, but all this did was enrage Ellis who ended up shooting Tucker's partner Pat Tate through his bathroom window.

Pat's house was even put under surveillance by Tucker's friend Terry, but unbeknown to him the police were also watching.

Despite this mad life Nipper eventually got his head down and into the books. Today he lives a safe and happy life in the Health and Safety industry.

Despite that kind of activity, there was also great camaraderie between certain factions and one night we found ourselves on the ale in a club run by another door crew.

They were complaining that they couldn't get the crowd of fifty or so punters from downstairs to leave.

This wasn't a problem for me and I offered to help. That help involved me taking the trip downstairs and letting off a can of CS gas.

Of course, all the punters immediately saw sense and made for the exit but what I didn't realise was there was also a doorman, Simon Wlikinson, down there who bore the full brunt of my 'solution'.

He made his way up the stairs, tears streaming from his eyes, coughing, and spluttering and generally not feeling very well.

As we fell about laughing, he failed to see the funny side of it. Well he couldn't could he? His eyes were chock full of gas-induced tears.

Altercations, conflict, violet encounters whatever you want to call them, have always seemed to be a part of my life, although I am not the sort to go out and needlessly inflict pain, fear, or torment on others. Some of us are just born into that kind of life, so even when I wasn't in the ring throwing fists, or guarding the doors there was always something going on.

On this particular night, my friend Porky and I had been on the ale and found ourselves in the usual nightclub. No good deed goes unpunished and in our quest for just a good night out, we found ourselves 'toe to toe' with another bunch of guys who apparently took a dislike to us.

As these mattes do, the issue was resolved without too many tears and Porky and I found ourselves making our way home, just chatting to each other, but fate doesn't always work that way and whom do we come across? Our foe from the club. This time their numbers had swelled and their two had become six. Porky and I didn't really give a fuck, outnumbered or not and I swear was like hearing the bell for the next round as we found ourselves at it again.

However, we needed something to make the match up and looked about for anything we could use for weapons.

Tough on us, right? There wasn't anything but my buddy was always good at improvisation and proceeded to kick down a wall adjacent to the bus stop.

Now we were talking, as we had a handful of bricks to throw at the enemy. As both sides enjoyed the battle (this is usually the case when alpha males hunt in packs) we were blissfully unaware we had an audience, also enjoying the show.

Once this audience had their fill of watching us they made their presence known the best way they knew how by turning on the party lights and sounding the sirens.

Whilst the other boys made themselves scarce, we tried to do the same, but Porky was a big old lump and we were caught quite easily. Sometimes that is just how it goes and sometimes you get lucky.

They charged us with criminal damage, nothing really to do with the violence they had witnessed and Porky? Well, Porky just wanted to go home and so when they offered us an 'out' with just a caution, time to go home, he jumped at the chance.

Me? I was different. No way was I having that on my record so out and out refused to cooperate. And so, I am led to a cell, my refusal adamant. After all, I didn't push the wall down did I?

So, I took my lumps and decided to wait it out but when you have been on the drink all night, eventually your mouth starts to dry and out and mine felt like the bottom of a budgie's cage.

Despite my pleas for a glass of water, they refused and I sat in my misery unaware that my partner in crime had charmed the guys at the front desk with his wit.

Whilst I am being the man from Alcatraz, Porky is sat out front, lording it up and making them laugh, all whilst drinking tea and eating bacon rolls.

As night-time turns to morning, the duty officer opens my cell door and gives me one last chance; take the caution, sign the paper, and go home or we take you to court.

Again, I refused and so with a sigh, he concedes defeat, opens the cell door and tells me to be on my way, no charges, no court.

I make my way outside and there is Porky in the reception, large as life, laughing his head off and smoking a cigarette.

Fair play to him, he had waited for me all night but I still told the bloody lump he had 'sang like a canary' to buy his cheap freedom.

Porky wasn't really like that though and remains, to this day a top man.

Another man I became friends with was Gary, and like most strong friendships, it didn't start out that way.

Gary Gordon and I met through a mutual friend, and he presented himself as Popeye the fucking Sailor Man. His massive arms were made bigger by an all-too-tight top and he loved to tell me how strong he was, so of course, it was always going to end up in a friendly fight. And just as friendships develop into something good, a friendly challenge is only ever going to escalate.

As well as bodybuilding, Gary came from a Kung Fu background and to be honest, I found it easy to pick him off as he closed in. My Thai-Boxing skills came into their own and tempers rose as the contact increased.

However, he soon became desperate and ran at me full pelt and out of nowhere, executes a perfect Judo throw, taking me to the floor but then landing on top of me and knocking the air clear out of my lungs.

With me struggling for breath and Gary's head

starting to swell from my strikes we call it a day and only then do I learn that his brothers Ian and Paul were both Judo players of the highest calibre and had taught him well, so well in fact that it started me on my own Judo path.

I was impressed by his throw, a throw I had never seen before and set about training with Ian and Paul, later having my own success in the Judo world.

Friendships are sometimes formed as two guys lie on the floor next to each other, battered and bloodied from the other's fists and this moment was no exception.

Gary and I went on to become great friends, taking on each other's problems with the law, and not turning our backs on one another.

Gary took an arrest for affray which allowed me to stay out of the papers and away from the boys in blue, something I really needed to do.

Things got crazy between us on a drive from our weekend away home when both worse for wear on the dreaded ale (read, pissed out of our heads), I decided to help him patch things up with his girlfriend by driving us back to her place.

The problem was we were locked out of our place in the sun which meant he smashed the door down to get our keys, waking the whole neighbourhood up in the process.

He didn't calm down on the drive up the motorway and dramatically acclaimed that if his girlfriend wouldn't take him back he would kill himself.

By now even I had had enough and offered to do the job for him by swerving our car at 100 miles per hour in front of an artic lorry. It had the desired effect. Gary sobered up, even helping out with the driving as he grabbed the wheel and steered us out of harm's way.

No mention of suicide was made again and in the bonus round, he did indeed makeup with his girlfriend.

And then there were the punters. If I make it sound like it was just trouble for the bouncers, our crowd of friends and fellow guardians, then that isn't strictly the case.

Without the punter there is no club, without the club there is no door staff and then you can reverse cycle that. So yes, the punters bought with them their very own unique brand of story.

Take the girl who comes in looking like a million dollars. She has spent the best part of the week's wages on nails, dresses and hair-do and why not? It has been a long week and Fridays are for the Friday people.

She alternates between a boogie on the dance floor and a shot of the good stuff and all we can do is watch on as it catches up with her.

Her end of the night will collide with mine as tired, weary, and just wanting to go home I do the last sweep of the club and there she is.

This girl who was a Goddess at the start of the night start now sits slumped on the toilet floor, knickers around ankles and caked in shit and spew. As much as I want to help her there is no way I am lifting her up. What, and end up smelling like her and covered in her fluids? I don't get paid enough for that but what I do is oblige with a container of freezing cold water over her head and the shock brings her around.

That, coupled with a stern warning to tell her to pull her knickers up does the trick, but she is still caked in diarrhoea and so myself and fellow bouncers hold her one arm each and walk her out of the club.

Sadly her night doesn't improve. The guy she is with runs at us mistakenly thinking we are having a go and he is here to save her graces. Unfortunately, his knight in shining armour act quickly disappears as he sees the state she is in and decides to save himself instead. He has worked hard for his money too and there is no way here shit is going anywhere near his new clobber. He pulls the old mistaken identity trick.

"Ahh, sorry chaps," he tells us. "My bad. I thought this was Sammy."

It is all he can do but to hide his disgust as he walks away, leaving us with the girl that is not Sammy after all. What the hell do we do with her now?

Make sure. We get her a taxi and home safely, it's all part of the job and being a decent human being.

Chapter Thirteen

By now readers, you may well have guessed that sometimes the world of the doorman can cross over quite easily into the criminal fraternity and that is what happened to two chaps who guarded Tots, a trendy nightspot frequented by equally trendy punters.

One of the doormen, Joe Wilks was involved in credit card fraud and whilst the origin of the attack was never quite clear, Joe was jumped on the way home from work one night.

His attacker, Matt B (who was also a doorman and involved in the scam with Joe), accompanied by two others hit Joe over the head with batons, putting the guy in hospital for a short time.

Now amongst the door community, there is a code of conduct, and nobody liked the uneven odds that Matt had scurried in his favour. Three guys with weapons against a solitary fellow guardian? That is a no-no and so I arranged a fair fight between the two. A 'straightener' some might call it.

These affairs are always done under certain conditions and as Matt also had connections, I went along as Joe's second along with my old friend Nipper. Matt of course had two of his buddies for support. One of the guys nobody really knew that well, but Matt's other guy was indeed a face, Mr Ricky Percival.

Now Ricky was part of the tribe known as the Essex Boys, the Next Generation and even had a film made about him, 'Bonded by Blood 2'.

To this day, Ricky sits as a convicted but innocent man, serving life in jail for a murder he didn't commit.

A man was murdered in an allotment in our local area, shot in the back of the head by someone who wasn't Ricky.

The man originally arrested for the shooting turned gave Ricky up for the crime, and so now Ricky Percival does the time. At the time of writing this, he still has ten years left to serve on his sentence, with campaigners still working hard to clear his name.

And so yes, you meet some big names whilst being involved in this industry. Anytime there is money involved, legit or otherwise you will find a 'name' not too far away and there was no name bigger than Carlton.

I met Carlton later on in the years and it was clear that Nipper and Carlton did not get on, at all. Carlton and Tucker were pals, men from the same team and Tucker wanted Nipper dead.

This didn't sit well with me as I was good friends with Nipper, and so I made a point of staying away from Carlton.

At this time, I was good friends with a guy we will call James and he invited me to add another skill to my growing talents; debt collecting.

We already worked together and the commission we would receive on the debts we collected would be a welcome addition to my door wages.

I would come to learn later that the debts were Carlton's to collect, but he had done his time and was now retired from active service, passing on the physical toil to others. It was still his show though, he was still the man with the connections and was the guy who could put the deals together and so we were grateful for the work.

In any business, any commerce there are the inevitable debts, legitimate ones, and ones that the debtor had refused to play ball in repaying.

These were the kind of people who ignored every letter that came through their door and so sometimes, other methods were needed. There is always a way to lean on someone to do the right thing and if they owed the money then they owed the money. Only sometimes they didn't.

We were given the task of recovering thousands of pounds from a local business and no amount of letter writing seemed to work and so a personal visit was our last option.

James and I made our way into the building and like anything of this nature, we were on our guard as we didn't know what to expect.

The only thing you can guarantee in a situation like this is that no matter who they are, the gatekeeper, the receptionist, the secretary, no matter who is our first point of contact will always give us the bum's rush, the knockback.

We were told to make an appointment but seriously? With the amount of money on the books here, no one is going to keep that appointment with us and so immediate action was called for and we made our way passed the willing front-of-house staff, barging our way into the owner's office.

If you have ever seen Rip Van Winkle, this is the sight that greeted us, this was our apparent 'debtor'. A seventy-year-old, frail old boy and the sight of him immediately changed our game plan. I mean, you aren't going to go heavy on an old 'un, are you?

He gave us what we expected, excuses, claiming he

had paid the debt over and over, but haven't we heard all this before? Except this time, it was true.

After producing paperwork to prove he had stumped up payment and more, we told him to get the creditor on speakerphone and we listened on, gobsmacked.

The creditor was unaware we could hear him, and the argument went on back and forth.

The creditor just laughed and admitted he had already been paid but wanted more, still unaware we could hear all this.

Turned out the old boy had even taken him to do his weekly shopping at a local Asda, stocking up the bully's pantry with all sorts of food and sundries.

Now say what you want about debt collecting, but nobody likes a bully and Carlton was no exception.

We went on our way, empty-handed and rightly so, reassuring the old boy we wouldn't be back. The bully? Well, Carlton spun the debt back on him, and it was he who ended up out of pocket, paying us all for our time. No one likes a wild goose chase, especially one driven by fraud.

Denial in the world of debts is as common and unfortunate as in the equally sad world of alcoholism. Nobody will admit to it until it is too late, and the latest adventure James and I found ourselves on would be no different.

Different day but the same script; "I don't owe the money."

This was followed up by the usual excuses that this was a different company, and that they were under new management. We cared not a fuck, James and I. Money was owed so money must be paid. You can liquidise all you want, you can put the 'spare comma' in between two companies' names to make them look like different entities but that money is getting paid, we were there to make sure of that.

Now you can sit down and make the debtor a nice cuppa, we know that tea solves everyone's problems from Irish pregnancies to family feuds and so James decided to put the kettle on, nice a friendly-like.

"I'll make us a nice cuppa shall I?" but I can see on James' face that the last thing on his mind is some PG Tips. If you have ever seen a man approach a kettle with a look on his face like James had at that moment then, well let us just say he was more excited than a big pile of exciting things and it wasn't the brew putting a smile on his manic face.

But the thing is, the guy isn't really in a tea mood and neither, does it seem is James. Seems he just wanted to boil the guy alive.

Readers, you get the picture and so thankfully did the guy who owed the money. We were paid up and said our goodbyes and all without the cheeky prick getting his hair wet.

On yet another collection we were sent to Halal butchers to get a return on someone's investment, but to say we were met with a frosty atmosphere would be taking the piss. The guy we approached was not the type to be intimidated easily, a cock sure very arrogant individual whose response to our presence was to phone the boss.

We waited patiently but our Spidey senses started tingling and sure enough, minutes later a car came rushing up, screeched to a halt and like something from a film, five heavily built Muslims exited the car and made their way toward us.

The fact that they turned up didn't bother us as much as the fact that each man carried either a big, fuck off knife or a machete.

And so after the usual stand-off, we chose our battles wisely and made our exit, but we would return to collect our money. It just wasn't worth becoming Kebab meat for.

As well as the quite obvious scary and dangerous

stuff (anyone coming at you with a machete is going to be dangerous, trust me), there were also the less obvious, more subtle jobs which carried their own worries.

Carlton still had a lot of connections and some of these were with the local Cash and Carries, the ones that sold the booze and goods at discounted prices.

Come banking day we were summonsed to their warehouses and went with the to the bank, our job being to carry their rucksacks.

Now these boys weren't going camping, and their bags weren't full of flasks and sandwiches. Instead, they were full to the brim with cash, sometimes hundreds of thousands of pounds. This was a worry because you never knew who was watching you, who had had a tip-off that the money was making its way through the street.

The owners didn't want to employ 'bob a job Securicor', but guys like us who, if need be, would fight to keep their money safe and that is what we would do if we had to.

Luckily that never happened, but there is no more sobering thought than walking through a busy street carrying the budget of a small nation on your back, all the time feeling like a fucking target just waiting to be shot at.

Still, man has to earn a living and sometimes that means a change of pace.

Chapter Fourteen

Just before one of the biggest events in my life happened, an opportunity came my way and I grabbed it with both hands as it was something that could potentially lead to big things.

A friend called me and asked me if I wanted to be an extra in a film and as out there as it seems, it really wasn't. I'd already done a movie, 'Rise of the Foot Soldier 2" as I'd been asked to by my associate Carlton. It was all bits like being in the background of certain scenes, looking the part and so forth but a great experience and so when this came around again and my friend asked me if I was in, it was a definite yes.

When I arrived on the set of Hooligan Escape, I saw that I already knew the lead actor, a guy named Chris Johnson. Chris was to play the part of a police officer and was a little concerned about his part in a fight scene.

Chris knew I trained in Martial Arts and approached me to ask for my help preparing him for a particular scene. The scene in question required his character to place someone in a Control and Restraint position and so the most effective and suitable moves I could show him revolved around wrist locks, arm bars and so forth.

One lock, in particular, is so effective that if the recipient doesn't comply, they either get a broken wrist or flipped to their back.

Chris loved it and wanted to learn it there and then. Of course, I was happy to oblige and spent some time teaching him as he was a very willing student.

It was a shame the same couldn't be said for his co-actor. Some things rely on compliance, none more so in the stunt world otherwise people don't get the move right and things look shit shaped. The worst case scenario is someone gets hurt but this didn't seem to bother his colleague who acted awkwardly and just locked on, preventing the move and therefore the scene to be completed.

Chris eventually gave up on the chap and approached me to see if I would step in and take the part.

Knowing how these things worked and having been involved in countless Martial Arts demonstrations I was happy to oblige.

As Chris performed the required mode I reverted to Judo and threw myself into my fall, going a little bit higher than perhaps I would have done for real, but the scene is everything in films and the crew loved it.

We ended up doing about a hundred takes from every conceivable angle, (they weren't the ones getting thrown, what did they care?) and the scene made the cut and was even in the trailer.

As the filming came to a close, I realised how much I enjoyed it and wanted more. After all, this could be a whole new career direction for me whilst retaining my Martial Arts training and putting it to use on screen.

I started looking around, putting the feelers out and came across a casting site online that was ideal for me as they were looking for actors who wanted to do fight scenes and stunt work. What better chance than this?

Reading further into it I was very pleased to see that a guy I had trained on seminars with when I was younger was involved. Mr Dave Lea had been a regular feature in Combat magazine showing off his very impressive Kung Fu and Karate skills.

As well as formal Martial Arts training Dave was the personal bodyguard to page three model Sam Fox and as impressive as this was, he topped it by becoming the stunt double to Michael Keaton in the Batman film and further went on to be in Van Damme's Double Impact and Demolition Man with Mr Rocky himself, Sylvester Stallone.

As well as being on screen in these ventures, he also had a role behind the scenes as well, training Tom Cruise, Sandra Bullock and Kurt Russell to name a few, so being on a stunt training event with him meant you were in good hands.

And so that is when I found myself, heading up the motorway from the big smoke to the northern city of Leeds for a film choreography training seminar.

I introduced myself to Dave and mentioned I had been on his seminars as a youngster. Our shared experiences and interest in Karate meant we hit it off right away and got on really well.

After the seminar was over, we stayed in touch. Dave jetted back to his home in Los Angeles well I was homeward bound back to London but there were regular emails and phone calls.

Due to the time difference he would phone me to catch up on things at ten pm. As I never got phone calls this time of night, I knew it would be Dave and so always picked up. Given his role and the nature of the contact, it became known, in our private joke as 'the Batcall.'

My first real stint of training with Dave was when he was back in England and teaching his seminars. He was staying in Knightsbridge and after the seminars were done for the day or any other business he had was taken care of, I would make the trip over to him to train together, just the two of us.

Dave was a really great guy and someone I got on very well with. He showed what a genuine person he was when he said he wanted to help me progress in the film and stunt industry.

Dave was as good as his word and one day I received a call from him (regular phone, not a Batcall) and he offered me a part in a movie he was producing, coincidentally enough a Batman fan film.

I was to be cast as a 'goo' a baddie and what a day it was. Great fun and brilliant to do, a real experience.

Dave and I stayed in touch and the taste of film work I had experienced up until now only led me to want more.

My next step in this new world was to get in touch with a gentleman called Mark Johnson. Mark ran an international stunt team, a good one at that and he asked me to go and train with them which was another level up again as I became part of the team, staying in it for many years.

I was given roles in scenes in various films which was brilliant because it meant building up my

IMDB credits. If you know about films, you will know this is a massive part of making your way up in this world.

And so that, for a while became my way of life. Imagine it?

"Today Lee, we intend to set you on fire," or "Lee, could you just climb to the top of that tall building and throw yourself off, please? You do know how to fall don't you?" I loved every minute of it!

Chapter Fifteen

People come into our lives, usually unexpectedly and they have a great effect on us. Joe Emmons was just that guy. I met him through my mum's partner, another surprise as he was someone I really got on with, probably the only one I ever did which was kind of sad because I was fifteen years of age at the time. Imagine that, well into your teens before a positive male role model enters your life.

Kev Moore was his name, a really good man who liked a drink and was a regular at the local social clubs. It wasn't long before I started tagging along and loved it.

Another guy fond of the ale was Joe's dad who was a good buddy of my now, stepdad. It was whilst I joined the two elders for a drink that I met Joe. We passed the time talking in the social clubs as the other sipped away the night, and later on Joe and would bump into each other at the various boozers and nightspots in the area.

Joe was at the age and frame of mind when he wanted to make a name for himself, and he was well assisted in his quest by his ever-present snooker ball in a sock. Thing is, as well as carrying it he had of fear at all in using it, hence his growing name.

I was now working the doors and Joe was taking regular holidays to Thailand. One of these trips was to Bangkok that change the way Joe looked at fighting. He was always into football, but his main outlet was Boxing and Judo. However, on that fateful flight he was sat next to a Thai-Boxer who would introduce him to the 'art of eight limbs.'

The guy was Danny Kendrick and he wasn't on this flight to go and sample the local fayre. No, his whole reason for this grueling journey was to go and fight, and with this kind of dedication, it is easy to see how he became a Muay Thai Champion.

However, with Joe's love of the bars and nightlife, a curious sort of deal was done; Joe would sow Danny the good life, whilst Danny would return the favour and take Joe training. It was a match made in heaven, with Joe taking part in his first Thai-Boxing fight within three short months of the meeting on the plane.

Fighting was in Joe's blood. Some people are born to kick a ball, others to paint a picture, but Joe's calling in life was to inflict pain on people in the ring and so it is no surprise that he would have his own 'Fight Club.'

Of course he would, if it was good enough for Brad Pitt it was good enough for our Joe.

I never took place personally, but the legend has been confirmed to me by people who did attend his mad venture.

That venture certainly did not conform to Queensbury rules but those who took part loved it.

The anticipation of having your name put in a hat, with no clue who your opponent would be until it was drawn out of that hat a few minutes later, and just like that you were off. Scraping, brawling and generally being a bit wild.

I'd see these guys around town, noses broken, hands busted and black eyes and they would try and coax me to "Come down to Joe's Fight Club!"

It didn't really make sense to me at the time to fight your friends, we were having enough 'physical' on the doors, but each to their own, and they weren't harming anybody else in the process.

As well as fighting Joe loved to travel to his love, Thailand. He would spend three months there, then return to the UK to work for a few months before getting the first plane back he could.

Whenever he was home, we would meet up and if there is one thing Joe did harder than fighting it was partying. We would hit the clubs, parties and anywhere a good time could be had. With him loving being the life and soul of the party, there was never a dull moment, and you could rely on him to bring the entertainment.

As well as partying together, we trained together with our main range being Thai-Boxing but somehow, I manage to persuade Joe to return to Judo. It wasn't something that went down particularly well.

A night on the mats is always tough. The Judo warm-ups are notorious in the world of Martial Arts, and the training drills equally so but this night proved a disaster for my buddy.

His partner for the night took him down with a fair throw but it went horribly wrong. Joe went one way but his leg refused to budge and stayed put. The result was sickening. As he landed he twisted his knee and broke his crucial ligaments.

The look he gave me when he realised he was out of training for quite some time will be remembered forever, but real friends don't hold grudges and we went on to open our own club.

Southend Muay Thai would go on to produce many title winners, champions, and awesome fighters that Joe and I were honoured to teach.

Then an event happened that would change not only

our beloved Southend Muay Thai but my life forever…

Some days you wake up and everything seems to go your way, but this day? Well, this day wasn't one of them. As most of us do, I tuned into my socials, this form of communication now a way of life for us all.

Instead of the usual posts, pictures of cats and dogs, who scored with who last night and who was indeed "here for you hun," I was greeted with photo after photo of Joe.

Now Joe was a big name, it seemed everyone in Southend-on- Sea either knew him personally but if they didn't they certainly knew who he was and so the sight of all these photos caused a ripple of concern. That concern was to be confirmed just a few minutes later when my phone started ringing.

I guess I answered it with some trepidation, the social media posts with his image were many and so of course I had that doubt, but it didn't take away the massive pain or shock I felt when I heard the news. Joe had taken his own life.

We can analyse these things into we are blue in the face, but sometimes it just doesn't add up. I couldn't get my head around the fact that my friend had done this, had thought things so bad he had no other choice, but of course I didn't know Joe was suffering from mental health problems.

I don't think many people knew what he was going through because mental issues are taboo. Only his wife Donna truly knew Joe's issues and did all she could to look after him, to keep him safe from harm.

I spoke to Donna afterwards, once the shock had worn off and she gave me more insight into his condition.

"People only saw him at his best Lee," she told me. "That was how he wanted it. On his bad days he avoided people and would shut himself away for days at a time."

I suppose Joe was carrying whatever he was carrying and didn't want that shared with anyone, but I was his friend and it is sad to know he what he was going through, and the fact he felt he had to do it all alone.

Some say the show must go on and it was my intention to make sure that happened. Joe and I had started Southend Muay Thai together but if it was up to me, then I would keep it going on my own.

I managed it for about a year, really giving it my best shot but honestly, my heart wasn't in it anymore.

Every session was painful without Joe, our friendship, and the banter we shared as we taught, side by side. It became a lonely place to be, not the high-energy, fight centre we had dreamt it would be.

I started taking lessons off, leaving the class in the capable hands of Simon, another good friend. The thing is, one lesson off became two lessons, then a week and then I realised I was missing two weeks at a time. In my absence, the students had grown accustomed to how Simon taught, it was becoming apparent that they now considered him their instructor and so after a year of much soul-searching, I made a painful decision and reluctantly stood down from teaching duties.

We merged with Southend Combat Academy and even though this was a great move, a couple of our students wanted to keep Southend Muay Thai's name alive, all to honour Joe.

They respectfully asked me for my permission and of course, I gave it. If that is what they wanted to do then who was I to stand in their way and yes, what better way to keep Joe's legacy alive? I was too soon realise that there was another way to keep the great man in our minds and that is how I found myself on a flight to Bangkok, all to fight for Joe's title.

Almost twelve hours sitting on an aircraft gives you time to think. A hell of a lot of time. My companions are two fellow Muay Thai guys, Mister Mark Swords and Mister Colin Burman and so the journey is made slightly easier with the company. However, these guys carry their own memories of Joe, he was their great friend too and I know they are desperate to win their fights, eager to do Joe proud and so the flight for us is slightly subdued.

My thoughts drift back to Joe, the man who loved to fight, who love to party.

It is bittersweet to think of his backyard gym, a time we spent training, laughing, and putting the world to rights.

The long haul also gives me time to think, not only of the past and our Southend history, but also the future and in particular the day ten days away from this one. My fight is on the 15th of February 2015 which is a Sunday and we all expect a lively crowd that usually consists of both tourists and locals, the latter usually baying for a foreigner's blood.

No matter, once I am in that ring it doesn't matter who is watching, who is doing the shouting. I am here to do a job and I will do it to the best of my ability. I am bringing that title home for my buddy, the one who loved our destination so much that he practically lived there.

Sleep on the flight is in fits and starts, the monotony is broken up by the meals served by beautiful Thai girls, and by the in-flight movie, although truth be told it is hard to concentrate on any plot other that the one that will unfold in the ring in less than two weeks. It is further broken up with muted banter between the three of us, all urging each other on but all knowing we have our own job to do.

I feel the plane start to descend, that weird feeling you get when you fly and know you are almost at your destination.

The chatter of the tourists on board increases as tables are placed upright, bags stowed and books put in rucksacks.

The plane tilts and changes direction slightly as it moves towards its home and then there is a sudden, unexpected drop that brings out yelps and gasps from the children and nervous smiles from the adults. Every flight ever has that dip, and I am sure it is the universal language between pilots to laugh at the punter's expense. Not to worry, this lot will have the last laugh in the bar tonight, two glorious weeks of sunshine, swimming, beer, and the fantastic Thai food that lies ahead of them.

Me and my weary travellers? No such look, all we can think of is that first punch from a Reyes leather boxing glove that awaits us and that will surely land with spite and venom.

The wheel splash down as the plane makes a successful landing and for seconds, everybody feels that relief of firm ground. Yes, there is that smattering of applause for a job well done by the captain.

We jet-lagged folk now shuffle to the front of the plane, shuffle further to baggage reclaim and then the always, for no apparent reason, heart-pumping trip through customs. My days of carrying something that might cause concern through this checkpoint are well and truly in the past but tell me one person that doesn't have a completely pointless pang of guilt as they are ushered to the next official. Even the kids look scared.

Job done, customs cleared, and we head out of the terminal and Jesus, the heat. We all take a look at each other and see the same thing in our eyes; "Let's hope it isn't this warm on fight night."

As the passengers disperse the airport making their way to their paradise I remind myself of another task I have at hand this week.

You see Joe had an apartment out here and with his dreadful death, it is still full of his personal possessions, things he had acquired during his second life here.

His wife Dona has asked me to clear the apartment out, we all know that o one we know will occupy it again and so someone has to do the deed. I am happy to help.

It is with trepidation that I make my way to his home, and even more worry when I turn the key in the door. Entering his abode, I realise I have no idea what to expect, that to find here other than the obvious Muay Thai apparel, the gloves, shorts, t-shirts, books and videos that he is bound to have collected.

I am instead, shocked and saddened by what my old friend has amassed during his Thai time.

As I go through is cupboards looking for stuff that Dona would want but home, I find box after box after box of mental health medication, clearly indicating how poorly my good friend was. It is a sobering and sad moment.

"Joe," I say to myself. "I wish I had known, I wish you had talked to me."

The time before the fight drags, as it always does. My body is in constant fight or flight, my thoughts forever arguing with each other. "Yes, I can do this," versus the inevitable and natural counter punch; "What the fuck am I doing such a long way from home, about to do battle with an enemy I don't even know, let alone have anything personal against."

But as every fighter knows, we must always try to listen to the positive, otherwise really? What is the point of us being here?

Training with a week to go in any fight is light, there is no point in destroying our bodies with hard sparring, ripping muscles with heavy weight or excess endurance training or flat-out running and exhausting the body.

All the hard work, the stuff that counts has been done back home in beautiful Southend-on-Sea, more beautiful now than ever because it is so far from home. So, we stretch, talk, walk, try and meditate, anything to keep in touch with ourselves but also to pass the time.

That time also takes turns in hurdling toward us at full speed, taunting us with how quickly the fight is upon us and then slamming its brakes on and crawling toward us, teasing and taunting us, as if to say "I'll be there when I am there. I dictate fight time." This can make it incredibly difficult to relax but that is what we try to do.

Of course, there are always site-seeing trips, but

really? Who is in the mood for a boat ride down a canal? The Flea Markets hold no attraction to us, not yet and as for the Grand Palace, that will have to wait until after showtime.

So, we pass the time as best we can and then without warning (so it seems) I wake up and the first thought that enters my headspace is this; "It is fight night. All the training has been done, and all the waiting for us is over, this is time to do Joe proud." Yes, there is that, even though just getting here in the first place is enough to do that.

As we make our way to the venue I remind myself this is not Britain. Despite the tourist accents of Liverpool, Manchester, and London. Despite even the presence of Americans walking the street taking in the sites, Europeans drinking in the bars, and people from around the globe taking in Bangkok, this is still just that; Bangkok and with it the support for my opponent, a local lad is partisan, to say the least. If I am going to come away from this with what I came for, then I am going to have to work for it. I'll make sure my opponent does too. Nothing comes easy but I don't give it away that way either.

We make our way to the arena and it strikes me, this could not be any further, any different to the venues I have fought at in good old Blighty. This isn't the Sporting Village in Basildon. There will be no fancy ring walk, no throbbing music ad no television crews that we see on the occasional fight card at home.

This is Thailand, home of the hard, tough Thai fighters, the intimidating rouse of the crowd, and the stares of the opposing coaches. The street hawkers, the stench of sweat, beer and food. The whole thing seems to be designed to put me off, although I know this is not true. This is just fight night and everyone who takes part feels the same excitement bordering upon fear.

But then I settle slightly and it is the oddest thing that creates this settlement. It is the sight of the ring as approach it. It is when I realise that it is exactly the same size as the ones back home, just six. point ten metres by six. point ten meters. It has the same four corners, the same course canvas under my feet. This sameness helps me to control my breathing, but then there is another twist to this Thai tale.

I hear a roar from the crowd and I am reminded of the huge support that has followed me from Southend-on-Sea, halfway across the world to see me bring Joe's title back home and that is exactly what I intend to do.

I take my seat to get my hands wrapped, a vital but sometimes unnoticed part of fighting. Get this part wrong and you are in for an early night. The skull is the hardest bone in the body and hitting it without protection can seriously damage your hands.

Forget what you have seen on television, what you have witnessed the heroes do in the movies as they dispatch one guy after another with crushing headshots. Try hitting someone on the head, unprotected and see what it does for you. It can shatter the ones very early on leaving you practically useless for the rest of the fight.

And so my hands are wrapped methodically but the strange thing is, I watch my opponent go through the same process as he sits in a sit just next to me. In Britain, hell in most parts of the world the fighters are kept apart until just before the first bell, but as I have said, this isn't the rest of the world. This is Thailand.

There is something else that causes me slight alarm. Not enough to send me into the wobbles, but enough to give it a second look. The bloody size of the bugger I will be swapping hands with, in just a short moment of time. He seems fucking huge, not the usual slim but athletic build of a Thai fighter. Definitely the biggest eater in his family. Still, it is what it is, there is a job to be done and I'll do it even if it means taking on King fucking Kong. I'll do it for Joe.

The wraps, the massage and the 'oiling up' go well

so it is now time for the Wai Kru. This is no laughing matter in this game and respect is both given and received. It is a crucial part of what we Muay Thai guys do, a ritual performed in the ring by both fighters, a Talisman of sorts. All this seems to take forever, and then suddenly it doesn't. Suddenly it is over so fast and the reason we are here is right in front of me. My opponent gloved up and was ready to go.

I don't even remember who threw the first punch, fighting does that for you. Imagine being in a car crash and everything happening at various speeds. Imagine being asked to give a statement straight after the fender bender and you can't recall any of it just the way it happened. Welcome to fight land.

I do now I settled into the fight and started landing big, heavy round kicks to my guy's head but he gives me a little nod and smiles.

"No harm done here, let's just carry on."

And so I do because it's what I do best.

If you know Muay Thai then you will know one of the most effective weapons is the low kick to the thigh. Whilst the skull is the strongest bone in the body, the thigh is the biggest muscle and if you have ever suffered a dead leg, you will know how debilitating this can be, so I throw a vicious one to my opponent's left leg and do I see him wobble? Yes, I think I do. Thank fuck because so far I have hit him with every shot and it's like swimming in treacle, but finally there is a chink in his armour.

I plug away, head, body, head then down to the thigh and there he goes again. His base is being chipped away and victory can be smelt, I can almost hear Joe screaming instructions and so I launch one last heavy round kick. Before my brave opponent can hit the floor, the referee steps in and prevents him from further punishment. I am not sure out of the two of us who is more relieved. Me at the victory or him at the ref's mercy.

I look out of the ring, to the Southend crowd equally delighted at my win, but I sense something wrong. I can't see very well, they are blurred. For an alarming few seconds, I think some damage has been done. The crowd are swaying and distorted as I watch them. And then the panic passes for it is not blindness, just tears.

Fighting can bring enormous pressure, pressure like no other. The build-up, the training, the critics and the fans. The walk to the ring, the first sight of your opponent, the first punch you take, all of it feels like you are in a pressure pot and so the release at the end of such a major part of your life can be tears and a fighter's tears carry no shame. They are as important as that first punch you threw and that last kick you landed.

I had won and I had won for Joe, these were Joe's tears.

And so now, now we finally get to join the holidaymakers. The dad from West Ham, happy after a few beers, but feeling far from home and his mates. The scousers, knocking back booze and having friendly banter with the Mancs, their foe from Manchester. This friendliness isn't always the case at home but what the fuck? They are all Brits together on this glorious Bangkok night, let's all have a sing-song.

We will join them to partake in our own beverage soon, these three warriors from Southend-on-Sea, but first, we must pay homage.

We must visit the temple and light a candle for our buddy. Our buddy who gave us so much, made us laugh, taught us hard and our buddy that in the end was so poorly that he, well you know by now what he did. It doesn't need repeating.

And just like that, our Thai journey, our Bangkok adventure is over. It is time to go home.

Travelling such a distance can be exhausting even if it is just for a jolly, but add to that the pressure of a life-changing fight at the end of that trip, and well that is a different thing all together.

The taxi arrives at your house in the early hours, and you know it is just an hour or so to the airport, so why does it feel like longer?

The queues, the fucking never-ending, ever-present queues. Tazi to check in, check in to passport control, passport control to the gate, the gate to the plane, lane to the country, the whole thing again. It is enough to get on a man's nerves.

Now reverse it. You have done your job and you are homeward-bound. That taxi to the airport for the flight back to your loved ones? Nice little trip.

The line to check in? Not a bother, but it is to the poor West Ham fan, his holiday over, twelve-hour flight home with a slight hangover and then work on Monday.

And that same flight you share? Well, a couple of beers and then bliss as you get your head down.

"Why couldn't I sleep this well on the journey out?" I ask myself.

You wake with a bump as the wheels yet again hit the tarmac and you know you are just a couple of hours from your hometown, the same town you shared with Joe and your comrades at the gym,

Southend Muay Thai.

Fast forward and you are indoors, the place where this all started. There are hugs and kisses for the family, a hot sweet tea and then the last piece of the jigsaw. You place Joe's belt and photo on your mantlepiece. You are both home.

Epilogue

I thought I was done, but I'm not. Not by a long shot and though the guy's skin colour might be different, his build is slightly bigger than the last guys' and yes the rules are different, but the intent is still the same.

He moves into his position, me into mine and we commence. The grip on grip, stance against stance, he pulls, I push. Eventually, something has to give, someone's skills have to come good.

Mine becomes the latter and my hand is raised yet again.

On August 28th 2022, exactly 2,751 days since my victory in Bangkok, I win gold at the Judo, London Club. Yups, I think this old boy has still go it. After all, it is just fighting, right?

Lee Mayo, October 2022.

Tattoos can mean something, or they can mean nothing. We see people with Tinkerbell, Mickey Mouse a sunset, and a full moon. These may indeed be works of art, beautiful craftsmanship that most certainly deserve a second look, and respect for the pain the recipient went through to get 'inked'.

However, there are the other types of tattoo people get, the ones that are born of a life experience, adversity, a love, a death, a birth or a life-changing event.

I can sum up Joe's life by reciting his tattoo here and it is an ink I replicated when he passed. After all, that one single tragedy, an event that touched so many of us, was the solitary factor in bringing me out of fighting retirement to cross the world and throw leather again.

His tattoo, one I now proudly bear are words that I live by.

Read them here;

"Born to fight,

Trained to Kill,

Ready to die,

But never will."

R.I.P. 'Smoking' Joe Emmons. Our friend, our champion, our fighter.

Some of the greatest characters I've met in my life left far too soon R.I.P

Mike Williams
Joe Emmons
Roy burn
Dave Lea
John Mayo

Author's note.

"Writing this story, helping Lee honour his friend has been an honour and even given the content, it has been a warm journey to undertake.

Taking an outsider's look at a fellow human being, who took me from when he was a very young boy, through all his trials, tribulations, tears, fun and laughter to fighting such a long way from home has been inspiring.

However, as good a fighter as Joe obviously was, Lee's success in the world of combat and martial arts should not be overlooked. They are as follows".

2nd Dan Black Belt Ishin-Ryu Karate.

Multiple English and British Champion.

3rd Dan Black Belt Kickboxing with over 30 fights.

10th Khan Grade Thai Boxing.

Light Heavyweight Champion, Thai Boxing Gardens Stadium, Bangkok (and the subject of the final fight in this book).

MMA six pro fights.

BJJ Blue Belt.

Ju Jitsu Orange Belt.

National Ju Jitsu Ground Fighting Champion.

Ju-Jitsu Stand Up Fighting, Gold

Brown Belt Judo.

Tae Kwon Do British Champion, Southeast

Champion.

Mool Soo Do World Champion

All styles London cup champion not judo

Let us tell your story!

WWW.SIMONMORRELL.COM

Paths

By

Lee Mayo

&

Simon Morrell

Was bought to you by
www.simonmorrell.com

&

Liquid Bullet Productionz

Printed in Great Britain
by Amazon